TOO MUCH LOVE IS NOT ENOUGH

A MEMOIR OF SILENCE OF CHILDHOOD SEXUAL ABUSE

ROSENNA BAKARI

ALSO BY ROSENNA BAKARI

Nonfiction

Original Sin: Understanding the Movement toward Female Agency

Tree Leaves: Breaking the Fall of the Loud Silence

Self-Love: Developing and Maintaining Self-Esteem for the Black Woman

TOO MUCH LOVE IS NOT ENOUGH

A MEMOIR OF SILENCE OF CHILDHOOD SEXUAL ABUSE

Rosenna Bakari

Karibu Publishing
Colorado Springs, CO

Too Much Love Is Not Enough: A Memoir of Silence of Childhood Sexual Abuse.

First Edition

Published by Karibu Publishing

Colorado Springs, CO

ISBN 978-0-9971699-2-8 (hardback)

ISBN 978-0-9971699-4-2 (paperback)

For every survivor of childhood sexual abuse in every part of the world.
May you heed the sound of your own sweet voice, waiting to be heard.

PART I

Somewhere today, there is a little girl who is "Daddy's Big Girl" in all the wrong ways. He evokes fear instead of love within her. Nonetheless, she will always act with courage. Somewhere today, there is a boy who will be called a "man" for all the wrong reasons. He will learn to talk like a man but never feel like one no matter how much he ages. In the name of love, someone caused that boy and girl to hate themselves. Still, they will confront a world of ugly and search for beauty in it. They will never cry, nor shed a single tear out of pain. They may learn to fight back the tears with their fists in another person's face, learn how to live with the will to die, or hide their sorrows in a bottle or a pill; but they will not cry because they know when the first teardrop falls, the floodgates of pain will open. I know that child.

CHAPTER 1

S ilence is not a quiet space, and letting go of the past is not a task. Healing is a work of art. I could no more let go of my past than I could make a picture appear on a canvas by using my mind. But I tried. Despite my effort to live in denial, take on distractions, or ignore the effects of sexual abuse, pain kept begging for my attention like a spoiled child. I cringed every time psychological triggers forced me back to the reality that pain has no place to hide forever. It would live within me until I excavated it from the inside out. I had to find my tools and chisel away at the pain.

When I mentioned to my husband my decision to write a book about living in silence as a survivor, he nodded favorably and without hesitation. His response felt like an affirmation of expectation rather than confirmation of support. You know, like when your child tells you they earned an A on the spelling test, or the meteorologist reports it will not rain on your Fourth of July picnic as you peer out the window at a sunny sky. Had I stated the obvious? I knew my husband wanted me to be happy and wanted me to heal. Still, I desired a conversation about how I came to this decision. I hesitated to force engagement with him at that level since either he already knew how or he did not care. He had witnessed my struggle for more than two decades and he walked beside me, even if he did not always hold my hand. He certainly refused to carry me, no matter how tired I seemed. I knew not to ask for more.

Ten years earlier, a post-traumatic stress trigger led me to my tiny three-quarter bathroom where I balled up on the floor in the fetal position sobbing in fear, regret, and profound confusion as my husband lay in bed equally confused as to how to console me. In the fifteen to thirty minutes it took for my anxiety to clear and the voices in my head to quiet themselves, I made the most crucial decision of my life. I decided to live openly as a survivor of childhood sexual abuse. As I lay despondent with disbelief that my mind and body could be possessed by the experience of a seven-year-old I had abandoned long ago, I vowed I would not, could not, and should not continue to live my life looking for distractions from the truth. I promised myself that by the age of fifty I would be free from trauma. I thought I would allow myself six years to repair the holes in my heart with acceptance and care and compassion for my trauma. I had not yet come to the understanding that healing is a lifelong journey.

I returned to my bed and curled up under my husband's arm, my sobbing dwindled to a sniffle. As he held me, I told him I could not live in silence anymore. I explained to him that the pain of silence had become too heavy for me to hold back. I insisted I could no longer live as the trophy wife who displayed perfection at work dinners and family celebrations. As the perfect mother who homeschooled our children and answered to the title of "doctor," I was tired of spending my life making him look good. On that note, my husband broke his silence. He expressed surprise and disappointment of my perception of his needs. He insisted he never required anything from me.

He reminded me of my choice not to work because I did not want our children in childcare. I decided to homeschool because I wanted to control the learning content and teaching methods of the curriculum. I became obsessed with my fitness when I began martial arts, which I joined to spend time with our son. My husband supported all of those decisions, and admired them, but he refused to take responsibility for them. He admitted to asking me to pursue my Ph.D. while he earned his, because he saw me as too intellectually gifted to be less credentialed than him. Furthermore, earning our doctorates together would provide practical job security for our family, even if I chose not to work. However, never in our relationship had he requested silence from me about anything, nor attempted to take away any personal choice. Never had he denied my experience as a survivor.

I disagreed. The strange thing about silence is that it can be silently requested, encouraged, and supported. Over the years, he had offered no active support to help me heal. He never considered that my being around those who had violated me might be an emotional hardship. He never asked a question about the abuse. If I lay in bed and cried, he would turn over and go to sleep or pretend to be asleep. If I asked him to hold me when I cried, he would readily accommodate with verbal support saying, "You'll be just fine." I had walked out of the TV room too many times to count during a movie scene depicting men perpetrating violence on women. I explained my hypersensitivity to violence against women many times, but he refused to acknowledge weakness in me. He would just continue watching as I went to use the bathroom or to get snacks from the kitchen.

His responses reflected his ideal vision of me as a beautiful, brilliant woman who could deal with anything. He refused to see me any other way. He and I both indulged ourselves in the misperception of my perfection that, eventually, led to the bathroom scene. Shame prevented me from expecting his support.

I met my husband when I was twenty-seven years old and re-establishing my independence. We had both begun jobs that year at the State University of New York in Oswego. He started in the summer as a residence hall director; I accepted a position in October as a therapist in the counseling center. I had recently moved out of my parents' house in Philadelphia, Pennsylvania after an eleven-month stay to get back on my feet. I used my parents' house as a refuge from a failed relationship and poor career choices while living in Rochester, New York. I had planned to live with them for at least a year to save money. However, I could not tolerate the family dysfunction or the denial of my rape by my oldest brother who still lived at home.

I had kept the rape a secret since age seven, and even kept it a secret from myself. To this day, I have no clear memory of my brother violating me. I have only three scenes embedded in my mind like still-life images. I have a blurry vision of myself napping on a couch, then on the stairs with white stuff on my upper thigh, and the last image of me crying in the bathroom. I remember no pain, no conversation, no physical movement. My mind retained the fear, and my body stored the trauma. I had been afraid of my brother since that day that I still refuse to remember. I embedded my fear in silence, which is the most dangerous space in the world. It is the most common space for victims and violators to meet.

When I left Philly, I had little money and no goals other than to live out my adult life without ever having to live with my brother again. I returned to Rochester and stayed with a friend while I searched for a job. Since I began work at the university in October, I missed all the new faculty and staff orientations and "meet-and-greet" sessions. The Black Faculty and Staff Committee extended kindness and held a luncheon to welcome me. A dozen members attended, my future husband Ron among them. I had adopted a look and attitude of confidence, in spite of my deep insecurities which, apparently, impressed him. However, I barely noticed him.

CHAPTER 2

Several months after my brother raped me, I met my father for the first time that I could remember. He separated from my mother and left her to care for six children, with me still in the womb. He never visited and I knew nothing about him. People who knew my parents for a long time often would tell me that I looked like my father. The day I met him, I felt certain he would have protected me from my brother, who would never have hurt me if he knew he had to face our father. Our dad was tall, dark, and handsome. His muscular build came from doing manual labor folding cow hides and throwing them onto a truck. He smelled a mean musty even though he looked good. I could not stop grinning when my mother introduced me to him. I had felt a void from not having a father around, even though my second oldest brother Scootie took on much of the parental responsibility. He dropped out of school to work to help Mom pay bills. He funded most Christmases so my youngest brother David and I would have new toys and the family would have a tree to decorate. As much as I loved Scootie, he could not protect me. I knew my father would; I could tell by the tone of his commanding voice.

My father returned to the house a couple weeks later, and our parents sat the family down for the big announcement. They had reconciled their marriage, and my father soon would be moving in with us. Dad returned several weeks later to take his place as head of household. He commanded respect from everyone in the house, but my older siblings resented his return as head of household and his new rules. How dare he just walk back into the home and expect everyone to forget he had abandoned us for seven years, they complained. They preferred his absence because they had no fond memories of him. I had no memories of him at all, and felt excited about having a dad around like the rest of my friends. His presence made me feel whole, significant, and safe. Well, it did at first, but that feeling dwindled with each passing year.

My father did not come home every night. He worked three jobs, so I rarely saw him. We honored family time every Sunday and he insisted we attend church. We had never frequented church until he returned to our family to live a good Christian life. He did not smoke or drink, read the Bible daily, and often quoted scriptures. He dreamed of pastoring a church one day. I never had alone time with him, and since he talked far more than he listened, after a while, I did not desire it. He cussed like a sailor, and his third-grade education never stopped him from displaying arrogance. My mother allowed him to lead and remained reserved in his presence, despite her higher level of education and intelligence. She covered all his mistakes and made him look as smart as he tried to sound. Other than going to church every Sunday, my day-to-day life changed little once he returned.

My mother dreaded getting us dressed for church on Sunday mornings with nine people sharing one bathroom. One person at the sink and another in the tub sped up the process. Sometimes two of us would share the sink. No matter what my father's motivation for the reconciliation, my mother unquestionably saw the economic benefit of his return. She promised we would one day move to a house with more than one bathroom. More important, she wanted a home in which race riots, gang wars, and KKK mindsets did not directly threaten the lives of Black youth.

During my parents' separation, Mom had moved us several times, from project to project, to keep my brothers out of trouble. Drugs, violence, and sub-standard living conditions marked the lives of many families in poverty. My mother vowed a better life for us. She participated in local marches and demonstrations to advocate for improved community resources. In spite of desegregation, there were streets where Black people could not walk without confronting danger. More than once, Black community members found themselves running for their lives going to or from the store at the top of the hill. Growling dogs warned us to avoid marked territory. Someone once pointed a rifle at my brother David and me through a nearby fence, which increased the speed of our foot travel. Mom would sometimes give us a time limit for our trips. If we took the long but safer way, we would never meet our time allowance. Thus, we tried shortcuts and repeatedly found danger, people willing to harm our little brown bodies for reasons beyond our pre-adolescent comprehension.

By the time my father returned to the family, my two oldest brothers were done with school. My brother Mitchell and my two older sisters, Bernice and Gwen, were in high school. They went to a predominantly white school as a result of desegregation, and had to take SEPTA, public transportation, to get there. Sometimes race riots broke out on the way home, and they hurried in fear with their friends. David and I walked around the corner to our elementary school. The year before my parents' reconciliation, my mother turned down a scholarship for me to attend private school. She thought I should remain in the neighborhood school.

CHAPTER 3

Three years after my father returned home we moved from the projects to a house with four bathrooms. My mother took James and me with her to view the house. The trip required three buses and took just over an hour. We still had to walk two long blocks when we got off the last bus. My mother spent half an hour at the house with us and then left me at the new place alone with James. I remember her sternly telling him not to bother me and my fear that he would. The sternness in her voice suggested a reasonable mistrust or a reprimand for past actions that made me wonder if she knew he had hurt me in the past. I did not know what he had done to me, so I could not express my fear of being left alone with him.

No one came to the house for several hours. I remained alone with James, and my fear filled every room in the big house that would finally fit our family of nine. There were four bedrooms, four bathrooms, a finished basement, as well as a garage and a yard. Not one room in the house felt safe while I was alone with James. I could find no distraction in the empty house, no television, no furniture, nothing but fear. If my brother walked in a room, I walked out and stayed as close as possible to one of the three doors that led to the outside. Eventually, I went outside to sit on the stoop to separate from my twenty-two-year-old brother. My parents finally returned around dusk with my siblings, along with the moving van. I ignored my mother's reprimand for sitting outside instead of waiting inside and cried because I had no idea we were moving that day, and no way of saying goodbye to my friends.

In the big house, the small bathroom at the front entrance protected our privacy, as visitors did not have to go upstairs. To the left of the hall, the large tree in the front of the house could be seen through the bay window in the living room. The dining room had an equally large bay window that faced the neighbor's house. Mom filled the window sills with plants and decorated the foyer with a fish tank full of small exotic fish. My father planted vegetables in the yard. Neither parent had ever shown an interest in nature when we lived in the projects, so this type of living felt different and sensational for me as an eleven-year-old.

The eat-in kitchen had a table that sat four people comfortably, although only David and I ate together most of the time. We used the dining room when we ate as a family on Sundays. If we had company, we used the fancy dishes from the china cabinet that stood tall in the customized dining room arch. A chandelier hung above the dining table, and a door in the dining room led to the finished basement. Mom kept the door locked because potential intruders could use the windows as an entry. My brothers climbed in the basement window on occasions to avoid reprimand from coming home late or inebriated. Family members frequently found themselves mistakenly locked in the basement when they tried to return from getting clothes out of the dryer, watching television, or using the bathroom. Mom kept the door closed when small children visited because the stairs presented a safety hazard. In spite of her conscientiousness, more than one child suffered the fall, and each family member took the express trip to the bottom of the stairs at least once. The left-handed handrail sometimes failed in our navigating the narrow and steep staircase.

Mom furnished the basement as a second living room with a dresser in the corner that held my brothers' extra clothing. Previous owners left a bar, but my parents did not smoke or drink so my mother filled it with random items she wanted to remain out of sight. A television sat on top of the bar, and the walk-in cedar closet off to the side stored coats, bed linens, shoes, and discarded or lost items in disarray. A half bath with a laundry chute connected to the second-floor main bathroom; at least weekly we had to use a broom to release the bundle of pants, shirts, socks, underclothes, and towels to complete their failed two-story parachute attempt. The items sometimes fell into the toilet that sat right beside the chute.

The clothes had to be taken through a second locked basement door to get to the laundry area. Another walk-in closet in the same room stored Christmas decorations, extra-large cookware, and an assortment of junk. The wash basin sometimes flooded because the clogged drain would not accommodate the wash load spin cycle. My mother spent many full days in the basement toiling over laundry, separating whites from colors, pre-washing the collars on dress shirts to look presentable for church, and waiting for wash cycles to end so she could hang the delicates and transfer remaining items to the dryer. She disliked going up and down the stairs so she would camp out in the basement all day, literally all day, sometimes for eight hours. She rarely carried the clean laundry upstairs, but would call for the nearest child to assist, often me.

The tall, leafy trees and cut green grass made the home feel serene and I dreamed of the day I would live in it safely alone with my parents and my favorite brother David. As the youngest of the seven children, I imagined my siblings would be gone long before me. Each of the oldest five children was one year apart in age from the next. My mother wanted no more than five children, but her method of birth control failed twice, which explains the three-year separation between David and my sister Gwen, and the two-year separation between David and me.

I advanced to fifth grade the summer we moved from the projects. My mother sent me to a school near her new job as a mental health counselor. The short distance allowed her to transport me if necessary, as well as easily attend parent-teacher conferences. My brother David attended school closer to the house and usually would walk home. Most of the time, Mom dropped David off at school in the morning, and then me. I caught public transportation home from school, as did many of my eleven-year-old peers. My older siblings had to take three buses to get to their high school.

The family treated David and me as "the babies," and our mother often took us with her when she left my older siblings at home. David and I entertained one another while we waited with Mom at the bus stop, walking through the grocery store, at the civil rights rallies, or picking up food stamps. Elders often spoke our names together; David and Rose do this, Rose and David come here, David and Rose sit there. We sat side by side in church and on the way to church in the back of the station wagon. Even inside the house David and I hung out together.

When I left home at seventeen to attend college, only three of my siblings had moved out; James remained. My oldest sister Bernice had moved to Texas with her son and her military husband. My brothers Scootie and Mitchell remained in the Philadelphia area with their families. David lived at home and worked menial jobs. My sister Gwen lived at home with her first-born child. James had fathered a child, but the mother refused to have anything to do with him. As I got older, the house felt smaller, and I gave up on the fantasy of living alone with my parents. I created an alternative path to freedom and applied to colleges located at least three hours away from Philly.

CHAPTER 4

$\mathcal{I}$ lacked knowledge about how to choose a college other than by its distance from my fear. My mother wanted me to apply to universities within the Philadelphia area, but I refused, as I had done with many of her demands over the years. None of the children argued with my parents. However, disobedience did not count as an argument or as disrespect. My brothers had demonstrated the art of rebellion well for me. Like them, I often simply ignored my mother's requests. My father rarely monitored our obedience to anything other than church attendance, and dragged us from church to church trying to build his reputation as a minister. I never showed him a report card or discussed college applications with him.

I applied to Widener College to appease Mom but knew I would not select a school so close to home. I applied to Penn State with the idea of being roommates with my best friend, Pam. I also submitted an application to Cornell University because everyone at school recommended that seniors should apply to three colleges to ensure they would be accepted somewhere. All three institutions granted me admission, but I sent my letter to attend Penn State along with my roommate request.

Pam and I met in Spanish class in ninth grade. She took the class more seriously than most other students, including me, caring about education more than any of my other friends and earning mostly A's. I earned several A's but also received an occasional C. I honestly did not know the importance of the grade point average. Because Pam took Spanish class seriously, I did as well. We registered for the same Spanish course for the next three years, and had no other classes together, although we both played basketball and volleyball. I also picked up softball in the spring, anything to spend as little time as possible at home.

Pam ranked third in our class of six hundred seniors and I ranked nineteenth. Had I known the importance of GPA, class standing and awards, I would have been a better student. I knew nothing about higher education and had not thought much about college. In my junior year of high school I had classes with seniors and overheard their conversations about leaving home to go to college, which gave me the idea of leaving home. Most students at my all Black school were not planning to go to college. There were only whispers of aspirations, so Pam and I kept our plans between us. Pam appeared intelligent and displayed the character of a natural leader, whereas I acted like a follower and had a reputation as a fighter and being naïve.

No one in my family had gone away to college. My brother Mitchell and my sister Gwen had taken a few classes at the community college, but not consistent enough to pursue a degree. All my older siblings went to Roxborough, a predominantly white high school, due to busing and desegregation when we lived in the projects. David and I attended the new Martin Luther King, Jr. high school. We walked the two miles to school most days. A handful of students came from families that were wealthy enough to buy them cars to drive to school. Many of the students took public transportation from their more dangerous and less affluent neighborhoods, often using the free token subsidy. Only uncool students took the school bus.

Pam took public transportation to school and I only saw her there because she lived far from my house. Although Germantown and Mt. Airy are adjacent neighborhoods, the travel involved two buses and a half-mile walk after getting off the bus. I never had the time, money, or permission to explore the city for such a visit. My responsibilities at home had grown by the time I started high school, including cleaning bathrooms, washing dishes, helping with laundry, and going to church three times a week.

I looked forward to Spanish class because I got to hang out with Pam. We answered most of the teacher's questions and worked as partners whenever the teacher called for practicing in pairs. Like most of our classes, Spanish did not require any studying, only a few minutes working on ditto sheets for homework, which we usually completed before class ended. We often spent the last few minutes talking about sports. Pam encouraged me to try out for the volleyball team, which I did. Pam started on the team, and I warmed the bench.

I had problems with my algebra class, but not with the subject itself. Students were allowed ten minutes to transfer between classes. My schedule included a third-period gym, fourth-period Algebra I, and fifth-period lunch. Gym class required students to dress in gym suits, and the one-piece suit made a terrible fashion statement. It was ocean blue, loose-fitting on the top, elastic trim around the legs, and a pocket above the left breast. Most students did not wear the suit outside of the gym, dressing and undressing in a hurry between classes. In spite of the uniform, I loved gym class and often left last. The skilled movements of fitness made my body feel free, and gym teachers liked me because I never complained about working out like many students. Most of the girls tried to preserve their hair straightening. If their hair kinked during the week, they had to wait until Saturday to get it straightened back out.

By the time I got to the locker room and changed after gym

class, I had used up most of my ten minutes, and still had to travel to the other side of the school to get to Algebra. I frequently arrived late. I might have tried a little harder, but the teacher did not seem any more interested in being there than I did. He often sat in the back of the classroom after handing out worksheets for the day, and made little effort to teach us. I earned a B in the class the first quarter and a C the second quarter when my grade dropped due to tardiness. During the third quarter, the teacher warned me that my tardiness would continue to decrease my grade and I would fail the class if I could not arrive on time. He never spoke to me any other time, nor did he greet students or call us by name. I never saw him have a conversation with a student.

My behavior toward people reflected the way they made me feel. I felt quite insignificant to my algebra teacher, so the class became insignificant to me. I had already decided I could not get to Algebra I on time, and would therefore fail the class. So, I might as well not get there at all. Deciding that two lunches were better than one, I took fourth and fifth-period lunch most days. Usually I hung around the cafeteria or outside with other students who were cutting class.

I received a C- on my third-quarter report card for math, even after barely attending the class for weeks. I occasionally went to class if I could find nothing better to do. I still went late. I did not hand in any homework, but showed up on exam days for a while. Fourth quarter I stopped showing up entirely. The end-of-the-year report card devastated me. I earned B's in some of my classes, an A in Spanish and gym, and the C- in Algebra I stood. In spite of my willingness to accept the consequences, the teacher failed to follow through on his promise to flunk me, which meant to me that he had no reference for Rosenna Jackson. He never looked up to notice the students, and probably never graded a single exam. I felt as invisible to him as I appeared to everyone else around me.

CHAPTER 5

*S*ophomore year I advanced to Algebra II with Ms. Winston. From day one I knew my experience in her class would be different from Algebra I. Her desk sat two feet from the first row of students because she intended to learn each student's name and challenge their potential. This youthful African American woman commanded the students' attention and their effort to learn. She did not care about their feelings, only their minds. She referred to us as stupid when she felt our behavior warranted it and praised us when we did well. When a fight over a boy broke out between two female students, Ms. Winston got right between them and broke it up. She did not call the principal or send the girls out of class, but handled it just like a mom separating two children, then delivered a lengthy reprimand about fighting to the entire class. Her simplistic analysis that smart people fight with their minds, not their fists, set everyone straight.

I explained to Ms. Winston that I did not know any algebra because I had not attended the second half of the classes for Algebra I. Yep, she called me stupid for not going to class. She cared not about students' excuses, but wanted, and demanded, us to do the work. If we had to stay after school, come before school, or use our lunch period, it mattered not; she cared only that we learned algebra. I liked her and did not mind spending time with her, so I went to her during my lunch period and learned the work. She made time for me and I never missed her class because I wanted her to never have a reason to call me stupid again; I sought her approval and desired her respect. I earned a C- the first quarter. She expected more from her students and I kept trying to give her more. I earned a C+ the second quarter, a B- the third quarter, and ended the year with an A-. By the end of the year, Ms. Winston had taught me Algebra I and II and inspired me to enjoy math. She recommended taking Geometry the following year, and I accepted her recommendation.

Not all of my teachers that year cared as much as Ms. Winston. I failed tenth-grade biology after earning a B- the first and second quarters. I got along well with the energetic and kind teacher. Unfortunately, something happened and a cruel human being, disguised as an educator, replaced the original teacher. The new person continuously yelled and complained about everything students did, showing no kindness to students and no competence in any aspect of teaching. I came to despise her and hated being in her presence because of the harsh way she spoke. I stopped attending class in the middle of the third quarter, and my grade dropped to a C-. The fourth quarter I did not go to class at all, and my final report card indicated an E in biology.

I had never earned a failing grade in my life. My mother knew me to be intellectually gifted and became immediately suspicious of the school when she saw the failing grade. I told her I had stopped going to class because of the way the teacher treated students. My mother went to the parent-teacher conference and asked the mean woman for an explanation of the grade. My mother wanted information as to how my grade dropped from a B- to an E in two quarters. The teacher showed my mother the absentee sheet revealing my more than twenty no-shows to class.

Heat rushed through my body from fear and embarrassment about what my mother would do to me, and I prepared for public humiliation. Instead, mom ordered me to leave the room so she could speak to the teacher alone. I had no idea why my mother wanted to converse alone with the teacher.

I stepped out of the classroom and closed the door, but did not have to try hard to hear the conversation because my mother spoke with intentional volume to display her frustration. She scolded the teacher for her irresponsibility for my safety and academic progress. Mom expressed profound disappointment that she had not been contacted regarding the numerous absences of her child. Indeed, the teacher had made no mention to me or to anyone else about my absence. My mother argued she had never witnessed such unconcern from a teacher for a child; she never knew about the Algebra I class cutting because the teacher had given me a passing grade, and she would never find out. She threatened to have the biology teacher fired for her negligence. The teacher calmed my mother with an apology and a grade change to a D so I would not have to repeat the course. When they summoned me back into the room, the teacher apologized for not reaching out to me. She expressed confidence in my academic ability based on my GPA and performance in the rest of my classes that year. She asked for my commitment to be a better student by addressing classroom concerns rather than dropping out of class. I agreed, and walked out of the classroom, never seeing or caring about the mean lady again.

My mother had a lot on her plate, and I felt sorry for burdening her further. David had stopped going to school altogether that year, his senior year. Thus, his failure came as no surprise, although he disappointed me because I looked up to him. He had begun to hang out at night and refused to get up for school anymore. I would try to wake him each morning but gave up after a month. Maybe all of his teachers were as bad as the biology teacher. If so, I could not blame him for dropping out.

Mom could do nothing to get him to go. She had lost complete control over her household by then. Her grown children came and went as they desired. My brothers always left the house in a mess, and my mother expected her girls to clean up after them. She even let her nephew Larry move in with us.

CHAPTER 6

I did not know my cousin Larry very well before he moved in with us, although his brother visited us frequently. My mother came from a large family. Some of the siblings still lived in South Carolina, but most had moved to Philly years ago looking for the better life that the north promised but rarely delivered. They all supported one another, and my mother would never turn away the son of her oldest brother. She had the most spacious home of all of her siblings, even if it had the most people in it.

My mother must have known Larry smoked weed in spite of his attempt to hide it. He often came in with glassy eyes and noticeably awkward movement, not to mention the distinct smell on his clothing. Mom could not have known Larry would offer his drugs to her two youngest children. The weed may have contributed to David dropping out of school. David and I often smoked the marijuana together, but he used considerably more than me. At ages fourteen and sixteen we began to grow apart faster than I could make new friends. I wanted to continue spending time with him, so I smoked with him. When we were younger, we often played chess, basketball, cards, and board games. I followed him around, and he did not mind until I started high school, and he became serious about girls.

James also frequently came home high or drunk, but I never voluntarily interacted with him. Larry gave me joints to share with my friends when he dropped me off at school some mornings. I shared them with my class-cutting friends to help me fit in, even though I did not come close to a sense of belonging. There were only a few of us who knew how to get drugs, which made me valuable. I would take one or two puffs and relinquish the joint to the group.

I soon realized the joints were not free. The acceptance of drugs from Larry bonded us in secrecy; one secret begets another. When Larry began to molest me, I could tell no one. Because he did not tell my mother about my drug use, I could not tell her he put his hands on me. He never had to request secrecy, as I knew I could not speak of our interactions. I paid for the drugs with my silence.

I remember the first time that Larry touched me because I fainted during church service that morning. Mom ordered me to wake him to attend church while I searched the basement for my slip to wear under my church dress. When I shook him, he pulled me on top of him and put his tongue in my mouth. Later in church I went to the bathroom because I felt sick to my stomach. I asked my sister Bernice to come with me. Gently placing my bottom on the toilet, I doubled over from weakness and lost consciousness. I woke up disoriented, in more ways than one, with my mother at my side. After spending time praying for me, everyone returned to the congregation to finish service.

I never spoke of my morning with Larry. I had told Mom Larry would not wake up, instead of the truth that he had awakened and molested me. I did not have the words or the bravery to tell her without fear of blame. Today, such manipulation is known as grooming, but in the seventies, no one recognized childhood sexual abuse as a problem to be addressed, much less understood grooming. Women taught girls to behave themselves to avoid being caught on the stairs or in an alley or, in my case, in the basement by a man. Girls knew not to taunt; if they did not know, too bad. Boys will be boys. I knew silence would serve me better than truth. Of course, Larry had figured that out before he pulled me on top of him. He knew my truth would yield more restrictions and mistrust than I already received from my parents.

Larry's tongue in my mouth did not hurt as much as my mother's tongue calling me a nasty hussy, which she had done many times. Women frequently referred to girls as "fast" or "hussy" to criticize any display of affection, no matter how innocent, toward men; age did not matter. Ten-year-olds would not be spared such judgments if they sat on uncles' laps, nor six-year-olds who innocently kissed grandfathers on the lips. Surely, the eleven-year age difference between Larry and me would not have mattered. I would have been held accountable for provocation. Larry's hands in uninvited places hurt less than the threat of my mother's hand wielding a belt to tame my presumed promiscuity.

For two years, Larry molested me every chance he got. If he drove me to school, I had to kiss him when I got into the car. If we were in a room alone together, molestation occurred. His nice car, good looks, and charm frequently drew women to seek his attention. He brought dates home regularly. My body had much less to offer him than an adult woman, but that did not prevent him from touching me. He felt entitled to control my fourteen-year-old bony legs, knocked-knees, flat-chested body, not because I provoked him, but because he prided himself on his power to control females regardless of age or relationship. My mother did not allow me to have boys in the house, but she never paid attention to the men who lived there.

I tried having a real boyfriend in high school. I snuck over to his house one afternoon to have sex at his request, although I knew nothing about it. Fortunately, Larry had not forced me to have sex, but only touched me in intimate places. When my boyfriend attempted penetration, I freaked out a bit, not expecting it to hurt so much. After two minutes of trying, I chose to stop the escalating pain. If sex involved torture, I wanted nothing to do with it. I got home and called him on the phone to break off our relationship, and never spoke to him again. I could not understand why a partner would hurt you to express his care; sex did not feel like caring. No wonder people were supposed to wait until they were married and wanted children. My supposed partner called me for weeks asking me to talk to him, but I had no words to explain to him the disdain I now held for him. I blamed him for hurting me.

CHAPTER 7

I never got to live in the big house without at least three siblings still living there, but I had plenty of mall time alone with mom my last years of high school. We went to the mall on Saturday, mostly window shopping. We could not afford mall clothing but did plenty of free looking. We rode the bus forty-five minutes to the mall and made a day of browsing stores and eating. We bonded, uninterrupted, from the time we left the house.

Bernice, the oldest girl but the fourth child took care of me in the absence of my mother. If my mother could not take me somewhere with her, she left me with Bernice. Mom even let Bernice take me to choir rehearsal when we first moved into the big house. We rode three buses to complete the ninety-minute travel. Eventually, my family changed churches to be closer to home. Bernice and I still sang together in the choir, but I could walk the half mile alone, and Mom allowed me to go to church anytime.

Once, in a Sunday afternoon church service, the guest preacher said Christians who did not have the Holy Spirit were going to hell. Those who had the Holy Spirit prophesied in church, spoke in tongues, or did the holy dance through the aisles and pews during music worship. Many of the regular members, adults, and children, had displayed at least one of those gifts. I had none, and mostly sat in church waiting for the choir to sing and watching the clock.

The church never felt like a spiritual space for me. The people seemed no different from those I knew who did not go to church. God answered prayers randomly, if they were measured by the good and bad experiences reported during the testimony part of service. Within the church family and my birth family, no one exemplified God-like character to me. One's proclamation of their love for God seemed inversely related to their peace and joy. In fact, I had heard my share of sermons about how the devil begins to chase people when they profess salvation; their lives become full of challenges. Well, if God's will be manifested as suffering, I wanted no part of living within God's will. Perhaps that explained why I did not have the Holy Spirit. I never felt compelled to dance uncontrollably between the church pews.

In the middle of service, I walked out of the sanctuary and sat on the foyer stairs and cried. My mother noticed me leaving upset, and found me crying on the stairs. I explained my confusion and sadness about God and told her I did not want to go to hell for not allowing the Holy Spirit in my heart. She sat beside me and placed her arm around me and spoke softly in my ear. She told me she had no answers to my concerns.

My highly intelligent and humble mother never tried to impress anyone and did not lie with her words. I saw tears in her eyes as if she knew the preacher had done damage. In her maternal wisdom, my mother told me to talk directly to God. She told me to seek my answers directly from Him, not from man. She assured me I did not need to do a holy dance or speak in tongues for God to love me. He loved me because I loved Him.

Mom told me to pray and ask God for truth, which I did. I prayed that day, the next, and for years to come, for God to reveal truth to me and resolve my confusion. At the age of sixteen, I stopped praying for new clothes and a better life and began to pray for truth. My mother returned to the sanctuary and did not make me follow. She allowed me to stay in the foyer until the pastor dismissed the congregation. She had a way of showing compassion when I needed it the most.

CHAPTER 8

$\mathcal{E}$leventh grade began well. David decided to return to school, and I did not have to wake him up in the mornings. I left earlier and came home later than him. We rarely saw each other at school, but we did talk about classes. Mr. Metzgar, the geometry teacher, was tall, lean, and blond. His attractiveness did not go unnoticed by many of my classmates or by me, but his strait-laced, dull appearance and speech nullified all potential charisma. He lacked the fire of Ms. Winston to command a class, however, he did not need it. Students who took geometry wanted to learn and earn good grades. Most took only the required Algebra I and II math courses. Students in geometry intended to take the college entrance exams. I became curious about college from hearing classmates talking about the SATs.

Ms. Winston prepared me for geometry. I gained math competency and confidence. Equations taught me how to predict and the value of prediction. In my mind, I could make things work out if I understood the missing variable. Things should be the same on both sides, and I needed only to study the formulas. The simplicity of this strategy made perfect sense to me and I treasured it. I could not wait to see what geometry would teach me about life. Students had to walk past Mr. Metzgar's desk to get to their seat, but he stood at the door to greet us. I sat in the chair two rows from the left and four seats down with eyes wide open and interest high. Rosenna Jackson, the teacher called, mispronouncing my name as every teacher had done. I replied "Rose." No one called me Rosenna, nor did anyone mind the correction to Rose.

I warmed up to the teacher easily and enjoyed responding to questions and going to the board to complete problems. I did not care if I got the problem right or wrong; I liked the attention and having someone care about my learning. I did not mind that other students labeled me the teacher's pet. I took it as a compliment. I worked as hard for Mr. Metzgar as I had for Ms. Winston. I did my homework every night and arrived early to class to chat with Mr. Metzgar before all the students came into the room. I became over-protective of him. Eager for class to begin, I scolded students who took too long to quiet down.

Geometry diverged from algebra in that it focused on patterns and shapes, not only on numbers. The same principles applied. Patterns followed predictable rules that were consistent. Geometry problems consisted of "If" on one side and "Then" on the other. The "givens" fell under the "If" column and the conclusions under the "Then" column. Students had to use the "givens" to solve problems. The "givens" told me the size or shape of the patterns and perhaps the relationship of the shapes to one other. One cannot change the "givens" in the problem, but must use them to solve it. There is only one correct answer based on the "givens." The logic of math captured my mind and heart, and I wished life were that organized. I tried to make it that way, believing I could solve all problems in life as long as I had the right "givens."

Given that Larry was almost the same age as Mr. Metzgar but acted nothing like an adult, I knew that I should stay away from him. Given that Larry gave me drugs and molested me, he presented danger. I began to hide from him as I did from James.

Larry usually stayed out late, sometimes with David since he was now eighteen. They often came home after I had gone to bed. I could avoid Larry easily, as he came upstairs only to use the shower in the morning. I stopped accepting weed and rides to school from him. Fortunately, by the end of eleventh grade he had moved out of our basement and rarely visited. James, on the other hand, never moved out. I came to understand that he had a developmental disability, which made him my mother's dependent adult. His permanence in the house was another "given." I had to find a way to move out after high school to distance myself from him.

I did not know my geometry teacher would also coach the girls' basketball team. He was unaware of my interest in basketball. At tryouts, we were both pleasantly surprised. The coach from last year chose not to continue while expecting her first child. She taught, but transferred her coaching responsibilities to Mr. Metzgar, who valued academic ability as much as athletic skill. Most of the players he chose for his team had high GPAs, including Pam. He did not win many games with us, but he won our hearts. Some of the smart girls competed for his attention. I sure did. Mr. Metzgar would sometimes drive me home after the games so I would not have to walk the two miles. The other players lived farther and caught public transportation or drove cars. Mr. Metzgar and I usually talked about the other players and the game. We sometimes talked about my family, but I made it sound admirable. I told him how hard my father worked to support us and that he took us to church. I shared how much I enjoyed being an aunt and helping my sister take care of my nephew who lived with us. I talked about my brother David as my best friend.

Mr. Metzgar met my mother at the first parent-teacher conference of the year. They hit it off well because she liked hearing about her smart child. The rest of my teachers spoke equally as fond of me, but I bonded strongly with Mr. Metzgar because I enjoyed math and basketball. When teammates realized he sometimes drove me home, they started rumors about inappropriate behavior between us. Teammates questioned whether I earned my high grades during class or after school, and questioned my position in the starting lineup. I thought little of what people said about us, accepting that things were rarely as they appeared in my world. Lies and untruths were a part of life for me, for better or for worse. I appreciated that Pam always believed in my innocence.

At the end of the season Mr. Metzgar's wife cooked a big meal for the team. We cherished celebrating at his home, but no one liked Mrs. Metzgar's cooking. A kind woman, she thought nothing of inviting twelve Black children to her white neighborhood and offering us space to laugh and unwind with her giving husband, our teacher and coach. Mr. Metzgar coached volleyball, basketball, and tennis. Every team enthusiastically celebrated the season with his wife's terrible cooking. We probably should have appreciated her more.

I signed up for twelfth-grade trigonometry to spend another year with Mr. Metzgar. The first week into class he insisted that I should be in the advanced trigonometry class. We fought about it and I lost. He broke my heart and transferred me to the advanced level taught by an equally attractive white male in similar appearance. The teacher showed students courtesy and respect and delivered the curriculum comparable to Mr. Metzgar. However, he had never shown me how to box out under the boards, driven me home, complimented me to my mother, invited me to his house, or asked my opinion about anything. I had one year left of school, and I wanted to spend it with my favorite teacher. For two weeks, I sat in advanced trigonometry and did absolutely nothing: I did no homework, refused to participate, and failed a quiz. The next week the teacher reassigned me to regular trigonometry. I knew I disappointed Mr. Metzgar, and he told me so. Unfortunately, given the insignificance I felt in the world, I needed to be around someone who made me feel special. He was my algorithm for stability. He showed up every day and allowed me to cling to him. I saw him before school, during lunch, or after school. I performed to the best of my ability on the team and in the classroom. My jealousy of the other smart girls sometimes showed. They did not appear as needy as me, and he never gave them the same attention. Still, teammates noticed my envy and would rub it in.

CHAPTER 9

$\mathcal{T}$he mistakes of my siblings dictated the quality of my home-life. By my senior year of high school my parents had five grandchildren, and none of my siblings had married before becoming parents. David and I were the only siblings who had no children. Bernice married her baby's father and moved to Texas when their son turned three. I missed having my nephew Ryan around, as he filled some of the void left by David's decreased interest in hanging out with me. Gwen's baby's father abandoned her and the baby before she gave birth. Still living at home, Gwen placed the bassinet by her bed but somewhat neglected my new nephew. Depressed by the father's rejection, she spent most of her time sleeping. After Gwen got pregnant my mother barely allowed me out of the house other than to attend church. She required me to clean all four bathrooms, vacuum, and clean the kitchen on a regular basis.

Mom accused me of using drugs because I would sneak out of the house to have fun and spend time with friends, but I had stopped using drugs by the time she had become suspicious. She also accused me of being fast and having sex, but I had no interest in anyone touching my body. She could not see me evolving into a conscientious, success-oriented, future-driven honor roll student. Instead, she saw a hard-core child who needed to be confined and restricted based on my siblings' indiscretions. Mom demanded that I quit all after-school activity and come straight home after dismissal. I disobeyed and did the opposite, trying out for everything possible to avoid going home after school. I refused any restrictions from my mother other than what she had demanded of my brothers when they were my age. I never caused trouble with my disobedience. I just found it necessary for my growth and sanity.

Nothing I did at home seemed enough, and I could not satisfy Mom's suspicion. She once, without cause, called me in the house from playing with my neighborhood friends. The neighbor girls never got in trouble, and I could not understand her justification for separating me from them. I had completed all of my chores that day, and plenty of daylight remained. When I came in the house, she gave me no reason for her summons, but insisted that I remain inside. I threw my first tantrum that day, at age seventeen. I yelled and pouted and stomped upstairs and back downstairs and into the kitchen, still yelling about how unfair she treated me. I put my hands to my ears to drown out the sound of her voice as she followed my pacing.

I earned good grades, cleaned the house, stayed away from boys, and went to church. Still, I would never make her happy, and she denied anything that would make me happy. My brother David heard me shouting and caught me on the stairs on the way to my room. He quickly came to my mother's defense and demanded that I calm down. I did so on the outside, but not on the inside. I concluded that living in that house would make me crazy.

I felt sorry for Mom, not so much angry. She had to manage her unfaithful husband, drug-addicted son, and single-parenting daughter, all who shared our home, while trying to make us appear as a good Christian family. I understood her fear of me disappointing her and, at times, attempted to compensate for the disappointment of my siblings. I never wanted to let my mother down. I tried to ease her burdens, but did not know how.

My mom paid the most attention to me when I had fainting spells. She could not hide her grave concern. She loved me and wanted me to be well. The spells continued even after Larry moved out of the house. I would wake up to faint. I would walk into my parents' room and climb in the king-sized bed next to my mom. The answers to her series of questions were consistent: "No." Did my stomach hurt? Did my head hurt? Did I throw up? She felt my head to rule out a fever. Then she or my dad went to praying. Usually I fainted as they began to pray, and regained consciousness with little prodding. They never took me to the doctor for a medical assessment about the spells.

I cherished hanging out in my parents' room when I could be alone with mom. Sometimes I would just visit with her to lay on her bed after dad left for work in the morning. If she got out of the bed to pray, I would get on my knees with her while she petitioned God. Now and again I could hear her praying from my room and would walk in and kneel beside her. She prayed a lot in there and the room had an aura of spirituality in spite of the messy clothes laying around. I wanted so badly for God to take away her burdens and mine. She deserved better. I hoped God would answer her prayers. He fulfilled mine with acceptance to all three colleges.

CHAPTER 10

*B*y the time I received the acceptance letter from Cornell University, I had already sent in my acceptance to Penn State University. At school, the morning announcements included college acceptances and I heard my acceptance to Cornell University announced over the loudspeaker in Social Studies. I did not react, as most people paid no attention to the voice in the ceiling. I doubted if my classmates knew anything about Cornell University since no student ever mentioned the school.

Though the announcement went unnoticed among my peers, when I arrived at trigonometry class, Mr. Metzgar congratulated me. I told him of my decision to attend Penn State and he tried to discourage me from choosing Penn State over Cornell. I ignored him and he did not push. Word spread quickly among faculty about the student who turned down Cornell University. Every teacher I spoke with tried to talk me out of my decision to attend Penn State. One after another they expressed surprise, concern, and disappointment.

I could not understand why teachers were interested in my college decision. I did not hear similar conversations about other students' choices. Since I met my goal of going to college I did not understand why it mattered which college I attended. One morning when I arrived at school my homeroom teacher gave me a written request to report to the school counselor, although not my assigned counselor. I left homeroom following roll call, walked down two flights of stairs and through the long corridor, past the cafeteria, to find Mrs. Minkoff's office. I identified myself since we had never met. She got right to the point of informing me of her concern about my college decision and asked for my rationale. I explained my commitment to attend college with my best friend of four years.

With compassion, rather than disappointment, Mrs. Minkoff spoke to me about higher education, its purpose, and its promise. College should be chosen based on the opportunity for advancement in society, not based on friendship. People meet life-long friends at universities, in this case friends of their intellectual caliber. At Cornell, I would meet people from all over the world, not just the state. The professors would be more qualified and motivating, in spite of Penn State's stellar reputation. A state university could not compare to an Ivy League institution's offerings. There are only seven schools in this category of higher education. Cornell, an elite institution of higher education, should not be compared to a state university. My acceptance was like winning an Oscar, so I had to accept.

Mrs. Minkoff informed me that no student in the eight-year history of the School had attended Cornell University, her alma mater. As an alumnus, she had concerns about the continued lack of diversity at the university. As a guidance counselor in a Black high school, she also had concerns about the restricted opportunities available to students, and had requested that Cornell University recruit at the school. No other student applied as a result of their visit. I did not know why Pam or other students did not apply to Cornell, except most students did not apply to out-of-state schools. I applied because the high school paid the application fee.

Mrs. Minkoff asked me about financial aid, and I responded that I had received about fifty percent of my tuition from Penn State. I would have to take out loans to pay for the rest. I had not received a financial aid package from Cornell University since I had not accepted the admission. She asked for permission to contact my mother and phoned her right then and there. Mom answered and they conversed about our family finances when Mrs. Minkoff expressed interest in helping me attend Cornell. My mother explained that she and my father maintained the status of legal separation, so she received monthly child support in spite of their reconciliation. Mrs. Minkoff assured my mom that as a legally single parent, the financial package would be significant.

Within a week of my visit with the counselor, a letter arrived from Cornell University. I opened it to reveal a life-changing financial package. The university placed me in a specialized program to support minority students. In addition to academic support through a required summer program, the scholarship included full tuition, room, and board. The award required me only to show up and pass my classes. No work study, no commitment to play sports, no loans to pay back, and no higher GPA to maintain than traditional students. This package took the college decision right out of my hands; financial circumstances dictated my future. I felt sold to the highest bidder and did not experience the sense of pride that others felt in my fate. My mother immediately signed my name on the form and mailed it back to confirm my acceptance.

For all the rejection that I had felt in my life, the attention over my choice of college felt strange. Usually, only negative behavior, or suspicion of it, made adults notice me. I had experienced plenty of unnoticed disappointment over the past four years. I had tried out for the drill team my freshman year after I did not make the varsity basketball team. However, the leader denied me participation because I had knocked-knees, which prevented my heels from touching at a ninety-degree angle as required. The drama club accepted everyone, but few students got to act on stage. Disappointedly, I never earned an acting part. During my senior year, the honor society advisor insisted I pursue academics or sports, but not both. I refused to drop either and eventually she removed me from the honor society for missing too many meetings during basketball season. The advisors did not support multi-talented students. They wanted students who valued scholarship and I never valued it. In fact, I had little regard for the formal process of learning. Now, all eyes were on me and everything I did mattered. At church, I did not have the Holy Spirit, but now authority figures could not stop talking about me and praised me for God's show of favor. At home I became a family investment as the first child to attend college.

When I told Pam I would not be attending Penn State, she expressed disappointment and said she felt betrayed. Neither of us had planned for the possibility of separation. We had coordinated our applications and acceptances and now had to adjust to the fact that I broke our promise. Pam should have attended the better school since she ranked much higher than me. In fact, fifteen students ranked higher than me in my school. I wished one of them would have applied to Cornell.

CHAPTER 11

$\mathcal{T}$he buzz about college died down, and the stress of acquiring a prom date geared up. I did not have a boyfriend, although I had my share of crushes. I did not want a boyfriend after my failed attempt at sex in tenth grade. I liked a boy named Terry who I met at church. We talked often, and he would hang around the house a bit whenever possible without my mother noticing him. His sisters attended our church regularly, and Terry would come occasionally. After we became close friends he attended church more frequently. He asked me several times to be his girlfriend, but I refused. I asked him if he had ever had sex and he admitted yes. I feared he would persuade me to have sex with him and I would regret it and resent him. He pledged that he enjoyed our laughs and closeness and did not expect sex, but I did not want to feel the pressure if he changed his mind. I insisted on remaining friends and made a promise that I would choose him to be my lover one day when I felt ready. He called me silly, but I meant it.

Since I did not trust boys, I asked my brother to escort me to the prom. Most boys were very open about their intent to have sex on prom night and I wanted one who would not require sex.

My mother agreed that my brother David should take me to prom and I did not care at all what my peers thought about it. To my surprise, one other male showed up for me that night. I had told Mr. Metzgar I did not have a real date and why. Mr. Metzgar came alone, so we spent the evening dancing and talking together. My brother let me be while he blended in with the other few singles. He missed his prom since he graduated a year later than expected. He made up for it that night.

I had a great time at the prom with Mr. Metzgar. He talked about his children. He had a baby less than a year old. He affirmed my decision, no matter how forced, to attend Cornell University. He expressed great pride in the fact that his favorite student got accepted to an Ivy League institution. He said I set the bar for future serious students and comforted me by saying how much better off I would be when I met students as bright as me. He promised to keep in touch with me and requested that I visit him at school during college breaks. David and I arrived home from prom early enough not to cause any concerns. I remained safe in the company of two men who showed me love, my brother and my teacher.

Graduation came quickly. Students had to attend practice at the arena downtown and my father took me because my mother had no car at the time. The drive should have taken about forty minutes, but Dad stopped on the way, parked on a narrow street, and said he would be right back. He got out of the car and walked back four houses to ring a doorbell. I could see a woman answer and Dad walked in. Five minutes passed with me waiting in the car, then six minutes, and then seven. I panicked looking at my watch. He had told me to wait in the car, and I dared not disobey. I wanted so badly to knock on the door but feared what I might learn about my father, as well as what he would do to me for hurrying him. I waited another five minutes for him to return, and he had a different demeanor than when he got out of the car. Since we talked infrequently and spent little time together, I could not quite describe the difference, although he felt more distant than usual when he sat beside me in the car. I dared not break the silence between us.

The afternoon after rehearsal the doorbell rang. The mailman had already delivered, and relatives usually stopped by later in the evening. With curiosity, I opened the door. A delivery man handed me a long floral delivery box and stated my name. I took it inside to find one dozen long-stemmed roses with a small envelope addressed to me. I placed the flowers on the dining room table and opened the card to see Mr. Metzgar's signature. No one had ever given me flowers, much less long-stemmed roses. I beamed as my mother reviewed the congratulatory card, and she smiled as well. She liked Mr. Metzgar and appreciated him taking an interest in me. Receiving the flowers made me forgot about the disappointing morning trip to graduation practice.

Not all of my family could attend graduation because there were so many of us, which I did not mind. I wanted to see one person, Mr. Metzgar. Graduation lasted for what seemed like forever, but two hours passed on the clock. When the time came to turn our tassels, everyone popped up from their seats like bread in a toaster. Then the hugs and chatter began. Parents looking for their children, friends exchanging addresses, teachers congratulating students, and flowers being given turned the arena into victory chaos. I pushed through the crowd to find Mr. Metzgar. I fell into his arms weeping and he let me hold on while he tried to greet the other students. A friend of mine observed me crying in Mr. Metzgar's arms, which fueled her belief that we were lovers no matter how much I denied it. I immediately stopped crying so as not to feed into her perception. Too late. For years to come, she would tease me about his particular favor toward me and never let me forget that he bought me roses and gave her nothing, in spite of the fact that she played tennis for him for four years.

$\mathcal{I}$n a matter-of-fact tone, I once requested Terry put his hand on my breasts. "Feel them," I stated, unaroused with no interest in intimacy. My breasts outgrew the rest of my body just a few months before graduation. Neighborhood boys had teased me when I advanced to high school flat-chested, as if breasts were something I had forgotten to put on my school supply list. No cool ninth grader showed up to the new school without a fresh pair of tits. Some girls sported them like new shoes or a freshly pierced second hole in the ear. I had next to nothing to show; my breasts were just large enough for the inconvenience of wearing a bra if I could find one in my size. My sister Gwen informed my mother that my anthills with nipples had protruded enough for an obligatory bra. Mom agreed and went out and bought my white, padded cotton, thin strap, A-cup bra to cover my chest. Finally, real breasts just appeared like magic. I could not recall wearing a B or C cup. The day I asked Terry to feel my breasts, I had grown into a D-cup bra.

Terry laughed at the request. I insisted as I explained to him how uncomfortable they felt on my bony body frame. He touched them with his fingertips, careful not to burst them, but I wanted him to feel them for real. I repeated my request and he awkwardly groped my breast in a way that would not cause arousal for him and asked me why I disliked being touched. He wanted to know the reason for my lack of interest in physical intimacy, as if maybe he already knew. I told him I did not like it and did not have to explain it. I teased that if he went to church more often, he would know fornication is a sin. Terry never argued with my logic. He just loved me for however close I would let him get to me. I loved him back for not demanding anything.

Sometimes, not very often, I would sneak over to Terry's house after school. He lived less than a ten-minute walk from my school. I would visit on a day of early dismissal. Terry went to a school further away, so I had to wait for him to get to his house. I would only stay about thirty minutes, otherwise, my mom would reprimand me for coming home late. We would hug and kiss with closed mouths and lay on his bed or couch together. Sometimes we would just sit on his step. One day after school I went to Terry's house and his mother caught us hugged up on the couch that sat right in front of the door when she walked in. My heart thumped, not in a good way. I imagined her calling my mother. Instead, she angrily scolded Terry for having company without her permission and shamed me for being there. Since she had exacted the feeling of shame and disgrace herself, she had no need to tell my mother. Just ten minutes before, I had felt like a princess, but she made me feel like a whore. I never went to his house again.

Terry was a rebel in my mind because he did not attend church with his sisters. His older sister dated my pastor's son, and his younger sister had stolen my church boyfriend. That worked out well since I found her brother much more interesting. Sometimes when Terry did not attend church, he waited outside to walk me home after service. I admired that he did not feel threatened by God like most of the people in the church. He did what he wanted based on his conscience rather than deferring to God. I admired

45

that he did not care much about what people thought, yet cared deeply for me.

Terry knew our relationship would be different once I left for college. He wanted the best for me, although he would miss walking to my school to watch me play softball. He would stand outside the fence and wait for me to notice him. I would smile ear to ear when he caught my eye, but having him there did not make it any easier for me to hit the ball. My teammates would inquire about him, and I would claim him as my boyfriend. They would laugh and call me a liar, finding him too attractive for a simple girl like me. They also saw me too rough around the edges in manners to attract him. Terry had a high yellow complexion with "good hair." He had the slightest gap between his teeth and small almond-shaped eyes. He barely stood a half inch taller than me but had perfect body structure, not too skinny or fat. His good looks were another concern of mine. I thought no boy who looked that handsome would turn down sex for me. I would rather let him be free until I thought I could satisfy him. We promised to write each other, since I doubted his mother would allow long distance phone calls to me.

I should have let Terry touch me more. He had earned my trust, but the secrets I carried numbed my body of desire. I needed to be in control. I wanted to be the one to tell a man what to do and how to do it, even if I did not know. I did not want to be in the back seat of a car or an alley or on a couch watching the clock to make sure we had time, nor be on my back watching the door to make sure we were still alone. I also wanted to prevent having a baby out of wedlock like my siblings, and a handful of classmates. Still, I loved Terry and fantasized that I would show him my love with my body one day; that day never came.

CHAPTER 13

One week after high school graduation my parents drove me four hours from Mt. Airy, Philadelphia, to Ithaca, New York. I did not concern myself with the possibility of failure, as I preferred anything to the confinement and restrictions of Upsal Street. I thought college would be like high school with more freedom and teachers would instruct me on what to do, check my homework to make sure I did it, and give me good grades.

No one told me classes would have hundreds of students or professors would grade based solely on three difficult exams. Professors, to whom all students remained anonymous, assigned about fifty pages of reading per week, but could not care less if we did it. Most important, no one warned me that people did not want me there or think that I belonged based on the color of my skin. Had I been duly informed about any of these conditions, I would have been less enthusiastic about moving into Clara Dixon Hall the summer of 1980. Nevertheless, my scholarship required me to attend the six-week pre-college program.

The summer program was structured to prevent students like me from getting lost in the crowd when the regular fall semester began. We were supposed to make friends, familiarize ourselves with the campus, get to know our advisors, and get a feel for the academic rigor. I did all of those things, but had no classes with most of the people from the program because my assessment scores placed me at a lower level. Instead, we met after classes and shared movie nights in the lounge, as televisions were not permitted in the bedrooms. We had a dance or two on campus, and we learned to navigate the city bus system to hang out downtown on weekends. The two advisors for the program, Janice Turner and Larry Watkins, were responsible for helping us graduate in four years. They amended the "one out of three of you won't be here after the first year" speech given at our general orientation by assuring us of our competence and emphasizing the importance of asking for help.

Everyone in the program lived in single rooms in Clara Dixon Hall on the north side of campus. The facility had long corridors that stretched both east to west and north to south. Bathrooms were gender specific but large enough to accommodate more than ten students. Toilets stalls were separate from shower stalls and sinks. However, all the water pipes were connected. A flush would momentarily stall the cold water from the showers and subject the shower-taker to two seconds of scalding water. Students offered an obligatory loud "FLUSH" as a warning. Occasionally I suffered a burn from someone forgetting the pre-flush warning.

The threat of scalding water disturbed me less than the perceived danger of strangers entering the bathroom. Students who were visiting their friends used the same bathroom as residents. A flimsy plastic liner offered little privacy and no safety from potential rapists. I fearfully walked more than twice the distance to the bathroom than I did at home.

I wet the bed twice that summer and worried whether I would ever stop. Embarrassed and afraid, I had to carry the bed linen to housekeeping for an exchange. I made sure to ball the sheet carefully to hide the wet spot. I wanted to retreat from adulthood. The bedwetting, believe it or not, made me want to return home, as I felt unprepared on all levels.

My fear of the dark fueled the bedwetting. Growing up, Bernice would put me to bed nightly and wait for me to go to sleep before leaving the room. Sometimes she left before I fell asleep fully and I would become aroused with fear and call for her to return, which she always did. She also woke me to go to the bathroom at night. All three girls shared a full-sized bed, so helping me stay dry at night benefitted all of us. As I aged, Bernice encouraged me to use the bathroom on my own while she waited at the bedroom door.

When Bernice had her first child, she stopped waking up to care for my bathroom needs. I was thirteen years old and the bedwetting continued. Each time I thought I had the enuresis under control we would go on summer vacation down south to visit my grandparents. Sleeping in unfamiliar spaces triggered the bedwetting. No family member ever had room to accommodate all nine of us. We snuggled close on the floor or couches and crowded into beds at aunts', uncles', and grandparents' homes. The nine of us would be split between two or three homes, but my mother always made sure I stayed in the same house with her so she could deal with my problem. Even if my parents woke me to use the bathroom, I would still wet the bed before morning at least one of the seven nights away from home. I embarrassed my parents and they scolded me for it.

Bernice left home with her son and new husband a year before I attended Cornell. I moved into her old room and had a bed to myself for the first time, leaving the larger room for my sister and her baby. Gwen did not nurture me like Bernice, so I preferred being in my own room. However, my fear of the dark stole many good night's sleep from me. I always slept with my light on, pretending to read in bed as an excuse. Someone would turn it off at some point during the night after I fell asleep. If I tossed in my sleep and noticed the darkness, I immediately awakened fully and would get up and turn on the light. To go to the bathroom, I would first turn on the light in my room, step three feet into the hall and stretch my arm to reach the light switch, then walk quickly to the bathroom and turn on its light. I returned to my bed with all three lights on.

I did not anticipate the emotional distress of my developmental delays and doubted that I could push pass them along with the academic challenges. The counselor had lied to me when she said students at Cornell would share my intellectual capability; they were far above me, more like Pam. She should have been there, not me. I developed the imposter syndrome once I realized the status of an Ivy League school. Everyone I met talked about their goals and dreams and how hard they had worked to get into college. Some students attended Cornell as a consolation prize. They seemed unable to overcome the rejection of Harvard or Yale and continuously tried to prove themselves better than others. Most of the people I befriended wanted to be doctors, engineers, or architects. A few wanted to be journalists, and a handful majored in Africana Studies. I did not meet another psychology major the entire summer, feeling even more like a fish out of water.

For the first time, I wondered whether the doctors had correctly diagnosed me as mildly retarded at age seven. I had experienced a seizure and my mother took me to the hospital where doctors pasted electrodes to my wooly haired head to monitor my brain waves. They told her my brain waves were mildly abnormal and I would not be a typical learner. They gave her a bottle of pills to prevent further seizures and she gave them to me for about one week before noticing a drastic change in my alertness. She threw the pills away, hoping I would return to my usual self. Apparently, I did, because the school contacted my mother the next year to offer me a scholarship to attend private school.

In 1970 schools remained primarily segregated despite the

Brown v. Board of Education case that ruled segregated schools as unconstitutional. Special programs targeted specific students to desegregate schools. In some cases, economically disadvantaged Black children who tested as gifted were selected to integrate the white schools. No matter how well-intentioned, the approach created more hardship for the Black community by removing the best and brightest of its citizens. My mother declined the scholarship because she disapproved of taking the smart Black children out of the community school to raise the achievement scores of the white schools. She had fought too hard for quality education within our community.

I never felt gifted, but also never experienced learning challenges. I enjoyed learning what I wanted and did not mind learning required subjects. However, I always preferred playing over learning. The playground, basketball court, or king ball in the driveway could distract me from any book or assignment. The school counselor advised Mom to accept the scholarship to maximize my intellectual potential. The principal warned her that keeping me in the classroom with children who were not as capable would lower my motivation, which did not matter to me because I never felt any particular motivation. I simply tried to do what teachers expected or required of me, no more, or no less (unless I didn't like them). When I got accepted to Cornell University, my mother confessed to me her sense of guilt about not allowing me to attend the private school. She saw my Ivy League college acceptance as a testimony that when God wants you in a position, no one can take it from you. She knew God would put me where He wanted me all along. I hoped she was right because I did not feel I belonged.

CHAPTER 14

The expense of long distance phone calls prevented frequent contact with my family, so I seldom spoke to them, and they did not visit that summer. No parents visited. I felt lonely for my mother in an unfamiliar way. During one of the rare phone calls home, I cried to her about the challenging classes and my loneliness. She showed no mercy and insisted that I give school one hundred percent effort. I contested that I had already given that much and wanted to come home and go to Penn State. Unrelenting, she responded with the imposition for me to give one hundred and ten percent. This new level of demand for my success agitated me for only a second, after which I was filled with honor. For the first time that I could remember, I felt that my mother believed in me. I interpreted her words to mean that failure could not happen if I gave all I had. She trusted the inevitability of success when I gave my all.

My mother was forthcoming with me about the necessity of my progress. She insisted that, as a Black child with limited experiences and resources, I must represent all other Black children with the same limits. No other students from my high school were ever admitted to Cornell, as well as no other children from my neighborhood or church. Out of the sixteen thousand students enrolled, only about five hundred were African American. My mother knew it because she read all the literature the university sent to the house during the recruitment process. Thus, at the age of seventeen, I became an involuntary ambassador for Black America. My success was our success.

My parents picked me up from Clara Dixon Hall six weeks after they dropped me off. I left home as a high school graduate and returned home as a higher education icon of my community. I received accolades for achievement and advice for success. My mother planned for me to make my rounds to all the interested relatives, church members, and friends during my two weeks at home, but I wanted to see only three people: Terry, Pam, and Mr. Metzgar. I returned home to no restrictions and could come and go as I pleased. I caught the bus to Pam's house and hung with her and her family. Her father enjoyed cooking and invited me to eat fish and grits for dinner. Terry stopped by my house and also met me after church to walk me home. Mom did not fuss about me having male company.

Mr. Metzgar picked me up and took me to his house so his wife could cook dinner for me. I talked only to Mr. Metzgar about my fear of failure and disappointment about my miseducation. I told him everyone I met had taken pre-calculus or calculus in high school. We both knew my high school did not offer calculus due to the ninety-nine percent Black student population. The expectation was that students would not need or want to study advanced mathematics, or any other academically challenging course for that matter.

Not one class throughout high school had prepared me for the academic rigor of Ivy League education. I had no idea young adults who looked like me were so achievement-oriented. High school friends had accused me of "acting white" because I enjoyed Shakespeare, played chess, and volunteered to attend conversational Spanish classes on Saturdays. At Cornell, I stood out because of my informal use of language, unfamiliarity with classical texts, and limited academic knowledge compared to my peers. I expressed my frustration to Mr. Metzgar about feeling cheated out of an education. He listened with care rather than reminding me that I had rejected his attempts to push me further academically when he placed me in advanced trigonometry. He expressed complete confidence in my ability to catch up with my Cornell peers and to be successful. He did not tell me I had to achieve; he assured me I would succeed, and I believed him.

hen I returned for the fall semester freshman year, I chose to live in Ujamaa Hall. Students applied for residency based on their interest in serving the Black community. Similar to my high school, ninety-nine percent of the residents were Black. I felt at home, not only because the people looked like me, but because my mother had been a civil rights activist. I knew she would want me to be involved with the Black community wherever I was. Ujamaa residents were required to attend community meetings on Sundays. We discussed the impending revolution that the Hall Director always warned us about, learned about leaders and leadership and addressed campus safety issues. We planned community events and scheduled community service projects, including protests.

Ujamaa housed students by suites, which included two double rooms on either end and two single rooms between them. The six suite members shared one bathroom. Each unit door locked as well as our room doors. I had a roommate and felt safer than in Clara Dixon Hall. We got along well enough, but we were not best friends. My best friend was Susan, whom I had met in the summer program. She lived nearby in the hall for students interested in an international living experience. Susan was from Queens, but her parents were natives of Barbados. We had no classes together because her summer assessment scores placed her in higher level classes. She was a pre-med major with coursework focusing on the sciences. She was the smartest person I had ever met, more intelligent than Pam and I combined.

I never had a friend who wore braces before I met Susan. She had them removed when she went home after the summer program and returned to school wearing only her retainer. She, like many other students, wore name brand clothing. Her most visible sign of wealth was her portable typewriter. Most students had to visit the writing center to type their work, writing drafts by hand before typing them. Typing errors were messy and unacceptable to professors and Susan did not make them, so she never wrote drafts. She typed her assignments from her head and always received A's. In spite of our intellectual and cultural differences, we bonded. She took me under her wing and we formed a surrogate sister relationship.

For several reasons, I stopped hanging out with my Columbian boyfriend whom I met in the summer program. My mother met him when she moved me into Ujamaa. She greeted him politely but when he left she expressed her surprise that I was dating a white guy. I explained that he was Hispanic and I had met him in the summer program. That revelation brought her no solace. She did not forbid me from dating outside my race, but I felt pressure to make her happy. The other reason I stopped hanging out with him involved his choice to drink alcohol on a regular basis, which did not sit well with me since I would not turn eighteen and be old enough to drink until halfway through the semester. As such, I was not allowed in any of the campus pubs. Moreover, because I lived in a Black residence hall, a white-looking fellow roaming around to find me could create social barriers for me. Neither of us were comfortable with him being there. No space on campus welcomed diversity, so being together presented challenges to our relationship. We had to make plans to see one another because we did not hang out in the same places. Eventually, we stopped planning and stopped seeing each other. By the end of the semester he was dating a Hispanic student from our summer program and I began to scope out Black guys exclusively.

I had the freedom to explore boys, and explore I did. I found brilliant minds sexy and cared little about the outside package. I cared about boys' aspirations, intellect and kindness. Race separated campus life, but gender did not. Males and females hung out together and had co-ed sleepovers, partied, and looked out for one another. Ivy League boys did not expect sex from girls. Most of the freshman girls still bragged about their virginity, as did I.

My time with boys never tempted me into sex. I remained committed to holding onto my virginity until I got married and informed my suitors that I had no interest in advancing beyond petting. They never challenged or pushed too much, or threatened to be with someone else. We always hung out until one day we didn't. Eventually we would hear about one another's new partner through the campus grapevine.

One of the sweetest boys I met freshman year, Greg, majored in English and aspired to be a writer. He wrote short stories and poetry to express feelings about his life and passions. I met him at the Ujamaa Sunday community meeting. He grew up with his mother and older brother in the Bronx, living a modest life, while his father lived in Hawaii and ran a major company. His parents were divorced, and his father lived with his third wife. Greg received no financial aid because of the wealth of his father who, beyond paying for Greg's education, offered no financial perks. Greg did not wear designer clothing, drive a car, or buy extra possessions. He lived with humility and gratitude and struggled like most of the Black students.

CHAPTER 16

*D*espite the voluntary social segregation, I was unaware of the racial tension on campus until the midterm week. Exam periods brought out the worst in Cornell students. The campus tension, in general, felt like walking through a dark tunnel at midnight. To relieve some of the tension, students created primal scream time each night during exam week. Throughout the week campus students stuck their heads out of the windows and screamed for up to two minutes. Some white students preferred to target their tension towards blacks, using the display of Confederate flags, physical attacks, bomb threats and building fires in Ujamaa.

During my first semester, the fire alarm sounded around 1:00 a.m. and Susan and I stopped studying and cleared the building by exiting through the nearby fire escape, just steps from my room. We had a fire drill in Clara Dixon Hall during the summer, but not that late at night. Even though many students studied all night during exam week, a fire drill at that time seemed odd. We would later learn that someone had called in a bomb threat. I certainly felt threatened as we waited for the bomb squad and fire department to assess the situation. No one told me that white people detested our presence enough to kill us. I had not feared for my life based on the color of my skin since I moved from the projects. Hell, white people had urged me to attend Cornell University. Both the high school counselor who got the scholarship for me and Mr. Metzgar were white; I felt seriously conflicted.

I called my mother as soon as they allowed us to re-enter the building after finding no bomb. When I expressed that I genuinely feared for my life she explained to me that choosing to live in a Black residence hall would make me a target. She said it in a matter-of-fact tone to affirm my feeling, rather than free me from the situation. As a civil rights activist, she had experienced similar threats, placing her life in danger more than once by picketing and boycotting. I worried about the future of our country if white students at the elite universities chose to use their talents to practice white supremacy.

The Ujamaa hall director debriefed us at the next Sunday meeting, informing freshmen that threats of harm frequently occurred to Ujamaa residents. Many white people felt threatened by the Black brilliance that lived in Ujamaa. The future lawyers who would fight for justice, doctors who would cure diseases, engineers and architects who would build the tallest and most substantial buildings, and psychologists who would bring healing to our minds threatened the ideology of white supremacy. For those reasons, white supremacists did not welcome us there. After the first incident, I did not let it bother me as much. Every bomb threat, trash room fire, racial slur yelled or written in graffiti, and display of the Confederate flag fueled the Ujamaa community's determination to succeed.

The racism, academic rigor, and the psychological assaults caused Black students to rally around one another. Rather than relying on the university's Blue Light system for safety, we relied on each other. An in-house protocol existed for females and males to walk together at night. Black students who did not live in Ujamaa still hung out there but requested an escort back to their hall. The male students were obliged to offer their assistance. As most of us knew one another, finding a place to crash for the night was just as easy. We formed study groups, even if we were in different classes, pulled all-nighters as a community during exam weeks, and held a neighborhood watch for suspicious behavior. I began to bask in the validity of Black intellect as I watched myself grow into this role.

The 1980 presidential election occurred less than one month before my eighteenth birthday, preventing me from voting. Ronald Reagan, the former Hollywood actor-turned-politician who became governor of California, opposed the sitting Democratic president, Jimmy Carter. Reagan, a staunch conservative, focused on military strength. He had lost the 1976 Republican nomination but won it this time around. Black people considered Reagan a threat to civil rights and social justice, especially affirmative action programs. Black students held voter registrations and political discussions to ensure eligible students mailed in their ballots. During the election, we crowded around the Ujamaa television in the lounge. We watched with a sense of despair as Reagan won state after state after state. His historic landslide victory made him the oldest president of the United States of America.

Within minutes of the official announcement of victory, loud rumbles of excitement could be heard from the adjacent residence halls, almost as loud as the primal screams. Just as the reverberations faded, a loud voice screamed from a window, "Now you niggers are going back to the cornfields." Susan and I heard it as we walked toward her residence hall, and the words cut through us like a knife slitting our throats from behind.

The television miniseries *Roots* had shown America the horrors of slavery. The reality of elite white people wanting Black people to return to one of the most inhumane periods in modern history bewildered me. The white people expressed an insatiable need for power and privilege and ignored five hundred years of free labor with no reparations to Africa or to African Americans. They had a five-hundred-year head start on entrepreneurship, politics, higher education, and home ownership but they wanted more. They wanted me to be in a cornfield, to be someone's slave, subjected to sexual assault, hanging, whipping, and forced family separation with no bodily autonomy whatsoever.

I felt that no matter where I went or what I did, in some way, shape, or form I would never measure up. Someone would subjugate me and use my back to lift themselves up. The assertion bellowed from the window fondled me like a pervert's covert molestation on an over-crowded train; it was a psychological assault, a molestation of the mind.

$\mathcal{I}$ saw no reflection of Black culture outside Ujamaa unless I went to the Africana Center, isolated on the edge of campus. In my classes with less than fifty students, I was usually the only African American, unless it was an Africana Studies course. In courses with more than one hundred, the few Black students dispersed across the large auditorium. I enrolled in a Black literature writing class with Dr. Carolyn Whitlow to fulfill my English requirement. We wrote a five-page paper every two weeks based on the assigned novel, and were required to re-write any assignment that we received less than a B- until we earned the minimum grade. No student left her class not knowing how to think and write.

I earned a D- on my first paper as Dr. Whitlow demanded critical analysis and writing sophistication that I had not yet acquired. The first re-write received a C- and the second a B-. By then I was also working on the second paper and applied the feedback from Dr. Whitlow to my writing as best I could. I earned a C- on the second assignment, but had to rewrite it only once before making the minimum grade. My first five papers needed re-writes, but the sixth essay received a B- on the first submission.

The seventh assignment challenged all of the students, as we were required to write in "active voice" and without using any form of the verb to be or the words "it" or "thing." I earned an A- on this final paper, one of my most significant Cornell University achievements. Dr. Whitlow did for my writing what Ms. Winston had done for my math when I had arrived in algebra a grade behind. I completed the course with as much confidence and competence in my writing as in high school math. Writing became my saving grace as the remainder of my education I selected courses based on the percentage of the grade earned from writing assignments; the more writing required, the better.

I rarely studied or went to my lecture classes, as they were quite large and I felt invisible. No one cared if I showed up, so neither did I. I took few notes in the lectures I attended because my educational experience had not trained me to listen and write at the same time. The overhead projection slides were removed far faster than I could write. Most students read and studied on a daily basis but I did not because I had no knowledge of how to arrange the work in a meaningful sequence. The more difficult the tasks, the more I realized how undereducated I had been for the last four years. I possessed intelligence, but lacked maturity and preparation. I took two-hour afternoon naps daily while good students studied. Consequently, I pulled frequent all-nighters before assignment due dates and exams.

I dropped biology after failing the midterm and the lab work to that point. As the only Black student in my lab section, I felt intimidated by my lack of academic preparedness. The interactions between white and Black students were unfriendly, so I could not ask them for help. White students were competitive with one another as well, which attributed to the high suicide rate. Cornell University, reputed to have the lowest retention rates for students in the seven Ivy League schools, also had one of the highest suicide rates. No matter how much pressure my parents put on me, I could not take education seriously enough to kill myself. I finished the first semester with only twelve of my sixteen credits complete. My family and friends back home did not count credits, so I earned their support just for completing the semester. No one realized my shortcoming unless I confessed, which I did not. I accepted the accolades for finishing my first semester and told myself I would do better.

CHAPTER 18

uring my second semester of college I took an
introduction to psychology course along with twelve
hundred other students. It was the first course toward my major.
Students filed into the lecture hall every Monday, Wednesday, and
Friday at 10:10 to hear Dr. James Maas teach about human behavior. The chapter on human sexuality came toward the end of the
semester and I expected nothing different from this lecture than
from the others. I learned little in a lecture hall with over five
hundred students. Dr. Maas spoke explicitly about the biological
process of reproduction. About halfway through the lecture I had
a flashback. I stopped paying attention the instant Dr. Maas spoke
about ejaculation, as my mind was unable to handle the information that came at me.

Flashes of myself on the couch, the staircase, and the bathroom burst through my mind mid-lecture. I filled with shame as I
came to understand for the first time that the white substance on
my thigh was my brother's semen. I felt ill, and at that moment
had to resist the urge to scream. I knew James had hurt me, but I
did not understand the act of sex or rape. I had never seen or

discussed semen. When I tried to have sex in high school, the boy did not ejaculate because I stopped him before we got that far. No wonder I had no interest in sex. I wanted to call my mother to tell her about the flashbacks and ask if she knew James had raped me.

I did not have the nerve to mention the flashbacks to my mother. I usually called her on the Sundays I attended church, never on a Sunday I skipped, as I knew my apparent dedication to church made her proud of me. Our conversations usually lasted about twenty minutes after also speaking with some of my siblings and my father. I dreamed of more intimate discussions of truth between us when I heard peers talking with their mothers about boyfriends, birth control, grades, and their interests. I talked only about my responsibilities. I did not even tell my mother when I got my first period at twelve years of age; I told no one. During my third menstrual cycle, my mother saw the evidence on a pair of panties on my floor and questioned me. When I told her I did not know what to do and she realized I had been wearing stained underclothes for the third month, she shifted the responsibility of educating me about my body to my older sisters. She looked in the closet that I shared with my sisters and pulled out a Kotex and informed me how to use it. Then she gave me the sex talk, which focused only on the one hundred percent protection against unwanted pregnancy and disease, don't have sex.

I would never speak of the flashes to anyone. The memories seemed unreal because of the still images and I doubted them. Denying such a horror made me feel more civilized than accepting that life could be so cruel. I convinced myself that no seven-year-old could survive rape. Thus, something else must have happened. I would have told someone in the family because I was known as a cry-baby. A hundred family stories passed between the nine of us. David and I talked about everything, with no secrets between us. My sisters vented to me about everything they hated within the family. With all of this talk, at some point someone would mention the youngest child had been raped by the oldest. No one ever said anything about a rape in the family. Therefore, it could not have happened. I would have known for sure and remembered who helped me. Nope, the flashes were a glitch in my brain, I kept telling myself.

CHAPTER 19

I wanted to indulge myself in drugs and alcohol to suppress the memories of rape bulging through my consciousness. I could not afford the cash so I settled for the weekend nickel bag of weed shared amongst five friends, the cheapest bottle of liquor with the highest content of alcohol, or the measly single drink I could afford at the bar now that I had become legal drinking age.

I could have escaped into my academics or buried myself in books between reading assignments and research papers if I had felt less inadequate and overwhelmed by the quantity of work. I had no idea where to begin. I spent three hours reading one chapter without comprehending what I had read in any meaningful way. I thought I was learning, but grades showed otherwise. I rarely earned higher than a C.

I could have indulged myself in relationships like many of my peers. But I avoided boys touching me, even more so now. So, I relied on what I knew: religion and denial, which go well together. I found a church off campus and an elderly couple would pick me up for Sunday service and drive me home afterward. Once a month they would take me to their home for a meal before bringing me back to campus.

I never wanted to see my brother James again. I hoped to never feel the stain of that still image of semen on my bony inner thigh. If I did not see James, maybe the picture would fade like the rest of the memories. I feared that other horrible memories might lurk in my unconscious mind. Choosing denial required practice and commitment, but I could think only about the rape for at least a week. I felt thankful that Larry only molested me, not raped me. I recalled that my seizure at the age of seven happened within days after the rape. I assumed my mind had to find a way to release the trauma by taking away the memories. Good minds do what is necessary for survival. I worked on forgetting it all again. The words rape and incest were too ugly to be spoken.

The end of the school year approached, and I panicked about going home to Philly. I had barely survived the family drama during the four-week Christmas break. I argued with my mother because she thought it reasonable for me to clean the house. Five adults lived in the house every day, but Mom expected me to clean it entirely, including my brothers' room. I had a responsibility to pay my dues, show my commitment, maintain humility, and clean for penance. However, the chaos of the home could not be washed away. My father hardly spent time at home and my brothers ran the streets and never helped with anything around the house. My sister took minimum care of her child and left much of the responsibility to my mother. I did not want to be a part of the chaos and would not survive three summer months in this environment after having a taste of freedom. I described this scenario to my sister Bernice with a request to stay with her in Texas for the summer. I did not reveal my flashbacks, as I intended never to mention them to anyone.

Bernice empathized with my concerns, as she had similar feelings about the dysfunction before she moved away; she happily agreed to my visit. While at Cornell, I talked to her on the phone as much as I spoke with my mother. Bernice and I were much closer to one another than to our mother. I told Bernice about every boy I kissed, course I took, and exam I failed. She kept me up to date on my nephew's growth. Although she became pregnant right after high school, she eventually married the father of her child and made a good life for herself. She moved to Texas with her new military husband when my nephew, Ryan, was three years old. Those years at home were enough for him to become very spoiled as the first grandchild. I helped care for him and regarded him more like my little brother than as a nephew.

Bernice confided in me the plan she and Robin made to elope an hour before she left to meet him at City Hall. They wanted to marry before Robin left for boot camp. My mother threw around the term "hussy" and angrily expressed disappointment when she realized what Bernice had done. As soon as Robin finished boot camp, he sent for his bride and their son.

I missed having Bernice around, but Gwen and I bonded a little more since we were the only two girls left at home. However, we would never be as close as Bernice and I. Gwen once poured scalding water from the tea kettle on my scalp for no reason. She also reminded my brother David and me that my mother wanted only five children, which would have made Gwen the youngest. She had a middle child complex that made her lash out occasionally.

Bernice, on the other hand, protected me from everything and would never hurt me. I once lost my mother's change when she sent me to the store for bread. She expected me to bring her back the correct amount, but when I got home I realized I had dropped two dollar bills along the way. I stood outside, too nervous to go in the house. Bernice came home from work and saw me on the step. I told her I lost the money and she dug into her purse and pulled out two dollars to replace what had been lost. I could always rely on her. She relocated around the same time David began to spend time with girls, and I had to fend for myself. I missed her and longed for her nurturing.

CHAPTER 20

*S*pending the summer with Bernice signaled adulthood for me as I decided and made plans without requesting my parents' permission. Bernice took two weeks off from work to spend time showing me around the city. We went to Sea World to satisfy the kid in me, and I rode some of the kiddie rides with my nephew as well as the scary roller coasters. Bernice enjoyed going to open houses on the weekends to look at big fancy homes we could never afford. We would take pictures to pretend we lived in them. We went to the Fourth of July fireworks, attended an outdoor Lou Rawls concert, and went shopping. Our time together augmented our relationship. I respected her as my mentor and loved her as my friend, not just my sister.

However, I did not know the indecency of her husband or that her husband would coerce me into a sexual relationship and become my third violator of sexual assault between the ages of seven and eighteen. I viewed Robin and Bernice the same, as my elders and caregivers for the summer. We had never held a conversation beyond greetings, but my sister always spoke fondly of her husband. My family grew to respect and care for him considerably. Once my mother could get past the fact that my sister had eloped, she bragged about her military son-in-law. He had known me since I was twelve and had seen the way my sister protected me. He knew I had little experience in the world due to my overbearing parents and saw me as socially awkward and naïve, presenting himself as caring, fun, and nurturing, and as a happily married man who loved my sister and nephew. His predatory nature went undetected.

Predators are not good people who are provoked into doing bad things. They are dangerous ones who do good things to disguise and protect themselves. Robin preyed upon me from the day I arrived, perhaps from the day my sister informed him of my visit. He began grooming me with the first act of kindness. Grooming teaches the victim to be silent prior to the sexual violation. Before the victim becomes aware of the violator's intention, the predator has trapped or lured them into silence. The violator uses numerous techniques to make the victim feel like a "partner" instead of a victim. When grooming occurs, acting as a partner is the only way to survive.

Robin groomed with kindness. He and my sister worked well together as a team. He would cook dinner so my sister could hang out with me and took their son to events or did whatever necessary to make my sister happy. If I wanted to do something Bernice could not do with me, he would naturally offer his service. He would take me to the store or an outing and watch television late at night. My sister always went to bed by 10:00 p.m. since we were children. Robin would come out of their bedroom after my sister went to sleep to keep me company, declaring that he liked having someone to stay up late with for a change.

When we were alone he would ask me a lot of questions about myself. I would answer, enjoying the attention as I had done with many boys at school. We talked about everything and he asked me about my experience with boys. I told him I had never had sex and or any interest in sex before marriage. He expressed admiration in my proper Christian answer. At times, Robin would sit very close to me on the couch, and I would try to create space between us. Soon his leg would touch mine again, and after repeated infractions, I realized his intentionality in making our bodies touch. I had no idea how to respond as he reminded me of my cousin Larry. Eventually, he used his hands like Larry, which bothered me a lot. I would resist, careful not to create noise. I did not want my sister to be mad at me or wake up my nephew. I also did not want Robin to get in trouble either because I enjoyed spending time with him.

I also realized Robin would deny the truth even if I knew how to tell it. So, I just kept trying to fight him off. When anything else becomes more important than resistance, resistance fails. By fear, intimidation, fatigue, and manipulation, he inevitably crossed all ethical boundaries. By day he served as the loving husband, by night he preyed on me as the couch pervert. I could not wrap my head around the cognitive dissonance. As my elder, I should respect him; as my sister's husband, I should protect their marriage. As a predator, I should fear him.

The small, apartment-sized house had three bedrooms close together, a kitchen, and living room on one floor. I had no space to hide as I did from James and Larry. I feared Robin, but, I feared my sister finding out more. She loved and needed him so much, and they were a happy family. I could not end such happiness.

My sister returned to work after two weeks. The first day she left me alone with Robin he increased his aggression with fear. When I finished my shower, I turned off the water and stepped out to dry off. I grabbed the towel from the rack and wrapped it around my small frame. As I completed the wrap, the bathroom door flew open and Robin walked in. He snatched the towel off of me, and I stood there naked with embarrassment. "You're so beautiful. I have to have you." His words indicated a threat, not a compliment and triggered a freeze response in me. I stood still, fearfully frozen with my arms folded across my body to cover as much as possible. My mind, in that second, opened and I felt all the physical pain, psychological fear, and emotional trauma that had occurred at age seven.

I desperately feared what would happen if I resisted any further. I would not survive a violent rape experience, not twice. Something in me flipped a switch and I became someone else, the only person I could become to survive. I mentally calculated how many days I had left to visit. Give him what he wants for only thirty-two more days, and he will not hurt you. I created a simple algorithm for survival: count down the days until I leave.

CHAPTER 21

I had been punished for beauty many times. Boys who touched me uninvited and unappreciatively reminded me that my beauty provoked them. The strange man who pulled his car over to flash his penis as I walked noted my beauty. My cousin Larry told me how "fine" I looked. When my sister's husband burst into the bathroom and stripped the towel from my freshly showered body, he insisted, "You're so beautiful; I have to have you." Apparently, my kind of beauty was not one of reverence, a beauty not to be preserved or respected but to be captured and possessed. Like a rose stem snipped from its bush while waiting to bloom to awaken the season of summer, people snatched my beauty, selfishly, and placed it carelessly in a container to die alone.

I never resisted Robin after he burst into the bathroom. He touched me when and where he wanted. Sometimes with my sister walking just a step ahead of us in public, he would turn and kiss me. I had asked him to wait before he had sex with me because I did not know how to give myself to a man. He agreed to wait and maybe a day passed, perhaps a week. My memory is unclear of the timing, but, it eventually happened, frequently, and without protection. I asked if we could use protection and he answered no. The only solace was that sex never lasted longer than five minutes, and he would roll over and go to sleep, even though it was morning or the middle of the day.

Similar to the violator, I lived a double life. I complied as the captured lover by day and engaged as the loving sister at night. The eighteen-year-old responsible college student running from her past crashed and burned. She no longer existed. Robin told me daily that he loved me and I repeated the words back to him. Of course, I loved him; he was my lover. At least that is what my brain told my heart in order to survive. Separating the act from the emotion would only add to the trauma although, in truth, I was his victim and he was my violator.

The brain is in constant search for patterns and situations that are related. When grooming occurs by force, intimidation, or manipulation, the brain's signals become confused, which is the power of grooming. The violator narrates the ambiguity and mixed messages for the victim, providing rationales and rewards for what has happened. The violator directs the victim to behave in ways that are not in their best interest. Their body and mind begin to work in the interest of the violator, who delivers a consistent dose of blame and confusion. Victims may lie for the violator, comply with or initiate physical contact, as well as protect the violator.

Compliance is merely the victim's adaptation to their environment, an adaptation the brain provides when it perceives no escape. The victim's response should never be interpreted as cooperation or consent; it is simply survival.

PART II

Survivors carry the pain of the silence that is forced upon us long after the sexual violation ends and becomes our permanent shadow of sadness. Rather than crying, we smile when we are forced to share space with those who violated us because they are at family functions or roam our neighborhoods. We bite our tongues instead of speaking up each time we hear the violator's name spoken in kindness by those who are unaware or refuse to recognize the damage. We shrink into numbness, unable to grow into fullness when we accommodate society's expectation to let it go. "Let it go" means do not grow. The words "move on" invite us to silence, not healing. Lies, betrayal, manipulation, and violence need attention, not silence. Pain has a voice; mine could not be heard.

CHAPTER 22

*A*fter leaving Texas, I had two weeks left in Philly before returning to school. I did not call or see Terry because I felt too ashamed and confused about my time in Texas, as well as what to think about myself. I knew the person I became in Texas must not appear in my life again. I knew I had done something that must never be repeated. I could not explain why I did it and could not untangle the difference between rape, coercion, and an affair. No, I could not see Terry or allow him to touch me or ask questions for fear that, somehow, he would know what I had done.

I hung out with Pam and talked about our perceived differences between Cornell University and Penn State. She had a white roommate but suffered none of the overt racism I had experienced at Cornell. Paying for school presented the biggest challenge for Pam, while I attended on a full scholarship. I did not even have a summer job. Pam had to work to earn money for college, as well as take out loans. We talked about everything, except what hurt me. I mentioned nothing about what Robin had done to me. Instead, we partied.

Now that I had no curfew at my mother's house, I could hang

out at Pam's house as long as I wanted. Her brother or sister always took me home since I did not have a driver's license and Pam did not have a car. If I stayed at her house past 2 a.m. I usually spent the night and caught the bus home the next morning after her father cooked me breakfast.

As we both were of legal age for drinking alcohol, we spent little time in the house. We went to the clubs downtown to party and danced much more than we drank. We never left one another when we went out. Interested guys met us on the dance floor where we conversed about our out-of-town student status. Most would-be-suitors did not want to write letters to commence a relationship, nor did Pam or I. We enjoyed the company of men on the dance floor for several hours before heading to Atlantic City to finish the night.

We played the quarter slot machines and walked the boardwalk when we ran out of gambling money, hanging out late enough to arrive back in Philly just in time for breakfast at Pam's house. Spending time with her allowed me to feel like myself and I never felt a need to explain anything. She referred to me as her best friend even though she had three sisters all close in age. We talked on the phone a few minutes every day to stay motivated for our upcoming semester. We knew once we left Philly we would rarely communicate until we saw each other for Christmas break. The day before I left for school, Pam stopped by the house to say hello to my mother, who always requested that she visit before going back to school. By the time school resumed, everything felt normal.

CHAPTER 23

*B*ack at school, I waited for my period, since Robin had refused to allow the use of protection. I felt a great sense of relief when it showed. I told Susan I had lost my virginity over the summer and she assumed my consent despite the fact that my "lover" was my sister's husband. I had no words to explain the truth to her because, as Ntozake Shange so poignantly wrote, "A rapist is always to be a stranger to be legitimate." A rapist also is thought to use a knife or a gun, not intimidation and manipulation.

I did not tell Susan about James or Larry, nor tell her the truth about Robin. I never talked about my resistance, which seemed not to matter. Actions spoke louder than words, so my ultimate action had canceled out the word "no," as if I had not spoken at all. I had no ground to stand on to consider myself a victim and I would spend decades learning that consensual sex does not result in self-hate. Partnering does not leave you with nightmares and cooperation does not seek denial. To a rapist, any "no" response means "use more force and intimidation." In truth, "yes" only counts if "no" is an acceptable response.

The rape at age seven instilled fear in me, the molestation

during high school made me feel discounted, and the sexual coercion provoked shame from the bottom of my soul. I tried to hate Robin, but found no place within me to allow it to emerge. I needed to continue pretending I respected the man who took care of my sister. For months Bernice and I talked about my summer visit and how much fun we had together. She spoke so fondly of Robin and I agreed with her.

The thing about incest is how securely it protects itself. Reputation usually saves the violator. The violator has access to the victim and they remain bonded through silence. Sharing secrets is how intimate relationships are formed and maintained. The more secrets you share with a person, the closer you are. The bigger the secrets, the more intimate you are. As long as I kept the secrets between Robin and me, I could not hate him. So, I hated myself instead.

I had a single room in Ujamaa sophomore year. I cried there, prayed there, and also smoked weed in my room. Susan began dating a young man and lost her virginity and her focus. She talked about him incessantly and spent more time on West Campus where he lived, than in her North Campus residence hall. The twenty-minute walk between the campuses prevented me from spending as much time with her. I started hanging out with a couple of first-year students who did not mind getting high on weekends. I also spent more time with Greg, the English major from my first semester. He frequently stayed up late, which I liked because I slept poorly at night. I felt more comfortable taking naps during the day. I went to Greg's room at 11:00 p.m. or invited him to mine to study after my other friends left. We sometimes fell asleep together.

I tried to be a better student and earn higher grades than I did my freshman year. I attended most of my classes and did my best to complete all of the readings using the distributive practice study method to avoid cramming. However, I could not focus enough to study thoroughly and scored low on every exam. By mid-semester, I had to drop two of my classes, chemistry, and philosophy. I went to my philosophy instructor for help with the course, as I enjoyed the subject. He offered me nothing. The course required a critical analysis of assigned biblical passages. Unfortunately, my analysis skills were fairly weak. I dropped the class to avoid a failing grade on my transcript or jeopardize my grade point average. The chemistry course took place in a lecture hall with two hundred students. I sat in the back with little comprehension of chemistry concepts. I dropped the class after the first exam.

My mind began to fragment in order to accommodate the denial of the reality of my victimization and to continue to present as a promising young adult. I wanted no part of the person I had become to survive that summer. I did not know that person and had no desire to know her but she remained in my thoughts. I often felt sick, my stomach, my head, mono, a cough, a cold, my body, my mind. I had little appetite and hardly ate, which made me fatigued. One Sunday, I had a fainting spell in church and the usher escorted me downstairs to help me recover. After service, my elders dropped me off at my room. The campus physician could find nothing wrong with me other than stress. I cut my hair short to change my appearance and somehow it made a small difference in how I felt about myself.

Like a girdle worn to fit into the dress bought one size too small, I wore my silence, tight enough to make me look good as long as I did not care to breathe adequately. Like the six-inch heels that make legs look divine, my silence radiated a confident personal presentation. No one knew my discomfort of shame as I soaked in the accolades about my perceived beauty and brilliance.

I went home for Christmas break and tried to help Mom manage the house. I still crawled into bed with her, and she always welcomed me. Her unhappiness showed as she relinquished more of her power and control to my undeserving father. My father transferred the family's church membership for the fourth time in ten years, seeking churches that offered him a seat on the pulpit as a minister despite no clergy or denomination ever ordaining him. Sometimes he preached for the Sunday afternoon service although his hypocrisy always unraveled at church as well as at home.

David shared with me that he had run into a sticky situation in his dating life. He occasionally hung out with Dad to help him work, or just to spend time together. My father introduced my brother to a woman as a friend of the family. David hit it off with her daughter, and they began dating. When my father realized that my brother took a liking to the girl, secrets unfolded. Dad forbade their involvement. When David questioned my father's contention, he revealed that the girl was his daughter. Obviously, David could not date his half-sister.

My brother shared that our father expressed no remorse for his multiple families. He had fathered children with several women. My mother did not condone his behavior, nor could she control it. My father told David that having multiple relationships was a man's right, as long as he took care of them. He did not view his infidelity as hypocrisy or a conflict of interest for a church leader.

Before returning to school, dad required altar prayer time. He had an altar in the corner of their bedroom where he burned candles and incense. When all nine of us first moved to the house, he would wake us for prayer most Sundays. We would gather around the altar while he prayed, sometimes for up to thirty minutes. After the prayer, he reached for his oil, removed the lid, and tilted the bottle with his forefinger inside. He would with-draw his oil-saturated finger and mark a cross on each of our foreheads, then dismiss us. I now did altar call alone with my parents.

CHAPTER 24

*F*eeling wretched about everything else in my life, I drew closer to Greg the spring semester of my sophomore year. I clung to him as I had done with Mr. Metzgar. One night I said to Greg "I wanted you to be my lover," yearning to give myself to someone I could love for real. Maybe a real lover would wash away the stain of shame of adultery or rape, or sexual assault. I needed to do something to cancel out the experience of sexual coercion. Maybe choosing a lover would allow me to love myself.

Greg showed surprise at my request since we were platonic friends, but agreed. I told him I needed birth control pills because I did not want to get pregnant. He concurred and we went back to studying. The following day I went to the health center and the physician gave me birth control pills and instructions. When I saw Greg I informed him that the doctor's instructions were to wait ten days for the drug to get into my system. We marked the calendar for me to give him my virginity.

We met in Greg's room and he asked me if I was sure I wanted to have sex with him. I took off my clothes and lay on his bed. He lay beside me, and we began with a kiss. He coached me on what our bodies should be doing; I followed his voice. When he started penetration, I felt pain, and he must have sensed me wince or felt my body resist because he stopped. I asked him why he had stopped and he replied, "Because I don't want to hurt you." His response shocked and confused me. "Isn't it supposed to hurt?" Greg insisted we slow down so I could enjoy the intimacy and reminded me I could stop at any time. He would not continue if he caused me pain. I had a revelation that partnering brought pleasure, while being a victim brought shame and I experienced a rebirth. I felt like a human being worthy of care and tenderness. My mind stayed fully connected to my body for the first time while a man touched me. Indeed, I had taken on a lover. My body responded to the difference between consent and compliance. I fell in love with Greg, and I fell in love with a man's desire to bring pleasure to my body more than his own.

I fell hard for my lover and lost myself in him. I desired to be with him every second because that seemed more comfortable than being with myself. I wanted to marry him, and I told him so. I wanted to feel special forever to enjoy his love poems, the late-night chit chats, the dinner company, the laughter, the lovemaking.

After a few months, Greg, always honest, raised concerns about me becoming too attached. Before long he broke things off to save me from myself and to focus on his schoolwork. I contested with tears and a plea to give him more space. He denied my appeal because he had asked me to do that before breaking up. I knew I had no one to blame but myself. However, I understood love no other way.

Greg saved himself from flunking out of school by breaking up with me, but I came close to failing out in spite of our break up. I dropped two classes again that semester and earned a D+ in statistics, a required course for my psychology major. I should have had a command of academics by now, but I did not. Although I had a 2.2 GPA, I accumulated only fifteen of the required thirty-two credits between the two semesters of sopho-more year, and the university placed me on academic probation.

I found solace in the fact that I would have to attend summer school to catch up, which meant I had to spend nine of the twelve summer weeks away from home without going to live with my sister. I did not want to see anyone or anything that reminded me of last summer, being raped at seven, or being molested for two years in high school. I did not want to hide in my own house, help cook dinner for violators, or look at my mother every day and wonder if she knew what had happened to me.

I felt safer at school than at home or at my sister's house. I talked about my family as kindly as other students spoke about theirs. I feigned disappointment in attending summer school, mainly when I talked with my mother. I had learned to focus on fantasy when reality is too perverse. That axiom became my coping mechanism.

My summer school performance showed me that I had matured. I handled the coursework with ease, taking a three-week statistics class for my psychology major and a six-week elective course. I needed at least a C+ in statistics to apply to my major in the fall. To my advantage, only twelve students enrolled in the class, including one of my friends from Ujamaa. The classroom was similar to high school rather than a large lecture hall. For the first time, I felt stress-free and competent at Cornell. I sat up front, close to the blackboard and the professor, and followed every example on the board. If I got lost, which was seldom, I raised my hand immediately. Statistical math is about probability based on algorithms. Ah, my comfort zone. I basked in the knowl-edge of z-scores, percentiles, and norms. I enjoyed homework. I worked every problem, attended every class, and aced every exam. I earned the second highest grade in the class. The A in that course would be my first and the only one on my Cornell tran-script. I will always cherish it because it boosted my confidence.

The following year I calculated my course credits so I would have to attend summer school again. I did not fail or drop any classes. Instead, I registered for fewer classes. I did not care that my scholarship did not cover summer sessions and took out loans to pay for my summer oasis. I also enjoyed learning in small classes. By the start of senior year, I had caught up and was on target for graduation in four years, a remarkable feat. My remaining coursework consisted of seminars and independent studies. I went to most of my classes because my absence would have been noticed. The professors knew my name, which meant they would know if I failed an exam. Thus, I partied less and worked harder. I still smoked weed or consumed alcohol most weekends and feared one day the bomb threat during exam week would be real. I put the sexual abuse behind me as I indulged in sexual pleasure with kind gentlemen who never seemed to take me for granted.

I dated a different guy each semester to avoid attachments. I tried dating two guys at once, but neither my mind nor my body could handle the confusion. Occasionally they would come by to visit at the same time and the three of us would chat until one of them decided to leave. I did not prefer one over the other. I once made love to them both on the same day, one in the morning and one in the evening. I valued the intimacy, but not the complexity. To avoid that happening again, I chose one over the other and fell in love with him. We remained partners most of my senior year and for a short while after I graduated, my longest relationship up to that point.

The advantage of entertaining one lover is that it takes the mystery out of pregnancies. I took my birth control pills assiduously, making certain not to have children out of wedlock. But, I once missed a pill because it dropped on the floor and I lost it. As fate would have it, my period did not occur on the twenty-eighth day as scheduled, and I panicked. I explained the situation to my lover, and we discussed our options. I went to a public clinic for a pregnancy test. The results took three days, during which we nervously waited before receiving the negative results. The scare reassured me that I never would have more than one lover.

I did not expect to hear from my mother about having a pregnancy test. She called me and asked me if I needed to talk, informing me that a bill came to the house from the Birth Right clinic. I felt awkward. She kindly offered her support; no name calling, no anger, no frustration. I told her I took a pregnancy test and it came back negative; however, I refused to talk with her about sex or my relationships. We never spoke of the incident again.

During my last semester at Cornell, my partner and I slept together every night, either in my room or in his apartment off campus. We usually stayed in my room for convenience, as neither of us had a car. I gave him twenty-four-hour access to my room by leaving my door unlocked when I left. I liked having him around but refused to get too attached even though I loved him. We agreed to love one another with no strings attached. I broke up with him frequently to assert my independence and after a while he would just leave for two days and come back when he knew I would be ready to apologize.

One morning I woke up not feeling well. My partner remained asleep as I went to the bathroom. I sensed a fainting spell coming on as I sat on the toilet. I awoke lying on the concrete floor of the stall with no idea how long I had been unconscious. As I became fully aware, I noticed my mouth felt odd. I lifted my tongue to scan the inside of my mouth and noticed that my two front teeth were injured. I picked my weakened body up off the floor and returned to my room to wake my partner. I told him what happened and he helped me gather myself to go to the campus clinic. As always, my body checked out fine. The fainting spells previously had done no permanent damage to my body, usually only experiencing extreme fatigue for two hours. This time my two front teeth had to be replaced.

My partner, one of the most sought-after men on campus, was

attractive and charming, but not vain. I appreciated his gracious-
ness when I was without my two front teeth for over a week. I had
to settle for the cheapest service possible, which did not include
temporary fixtures while I waited for the replacements. I
remained out of sight as much as possible, but my partner stayed
by my side to comfort me throughout the entire ordeal. I valued
his friendship and support.

CHAPTER 25

I graduated from Cornell University in Ithaca, New York in May of 1984. My parents came for the ceremony and blended in with the mass of thousands of spectators at the one hundred and sixteenth commencement. I could not identify them in the stands, and they could not recognize me among the graduates. Still, we identified with the day's significance. I achieved an American dream while hiding a nightmare. A poor Black girl, once diagnosed as mildly retarded, once abandoned by her father, educated in an all-Black high school, graduated from an Ivy League school in four years. I mattered. No one saw my past, so my history mattered to no one but me, while I now mattered to everyone. I shared the dream with forty-five hundred other students, but I lived the nightmare alone. I assumed my success would always overshadow my pain.

My mother stayed with me in Ithaca the week after graduation as I had no plans to go home. I did everything possible to distance myself from her, and she did everything possible to get close to me. She met my friends, went to church with me, took me shopping, approved of my boyfriend, and proclaimed her pride. I responded from a place of shame that still hid within me, knowing her disappointment if she knew what I had done.

I told my mother I did not need her there and did not want to spend my last week of college entertaining her. She cried but stayed anyway. I knew no better than to let her cry, as I wished that I had known how to cry myself. There was, simultaneously, so much love and so much pain between us and I did not know what to do with either. The pain prevented me from expressing love, and love prevented me from revealing the pain.

CHAPTER 26

I started graduate school at SUNY Brockport one week after graduation from Cornell University not knowing what to expect from an experiential counseling program. Attending the program meant I would not have to go home after graduation. Another twenty-one-year-old female and I were the youngest participants in the twelve-month program. The program began with a summer internship, which trained us to serve as academic advisors for the incoming freshmen and required two semesters of courses that began in the fall.

I learned the meaning of "experiential" the first day of "Groups," the course that introduced us to the dynamics of group therapy. Students played the client role for all therapy courses. For two semesters, we participated in mandatory counseling designed as coursework. The program sought to make good therapists by training students how to be good clients.

As clients, we learned to respect vulnerability. The classes also provided an opportunity for us to work through our emotional issues, because we needed to be healthy enough to serve as a healing resource for others. As a future therapist, we had to ensure our pain would not interfere with the therapeutic process.

I felt I had mastered moving beyond pain but was unaware of the difference between hiding pain and healing pain.

Eight students comprised my cohort of future therapists training to specialize in counseling people of color. Our advising responsibility included a caseload of thirty-two "at-risk" students. We worked twenty hours a week, simultaneously taking twelve credit hours of coursework each semester to complete the twelve-month program.

The two elective courses were exam-driven, with objective tests I could pass with flying colors. By the time I graduated from Cornell, I knew nothing in my life would be harder, at least not as far as academics. In four years, I had learned to study, think, and write. I understood the difference between subjective and objective tests and how to pass them. I learned when to write in the first, second or third person as well as the essential difference between writing research and opinion. Most important, I learned no matter how far behind I began anything, I found a way to catch up. Graduate school did not intimidate me at all. I anticipated no difficulties beyond my ability to pass exams.

By the time fall semester got underway, I was fighting off advances from the supervisor of our required internship. More than a decade older than us, he would use any excuse to get the two young students into his office to make sexual advances that included invitations to meet after work, comments about our bodies, questions about how we spent our time, or an invasion of physical space by standing too close for comfort.

The fear of walking a tightrope around men is exhausting, with no way to avoid a hostile encounter with those who want to possess you. A request for intimacy is never an invitation; it is more similar to a stick-up. Someone comes up from behind and sticks a weapon in your face, asking you for your wallet; when they find the wallet empty, you immediately begin to explain the reason it is bare to prevent retaliation with violence. The other young student and I strategized and negotiated our physical space around the office to be sure we would graduate and receive good recommendations.

Group Therapy class, the Achilles heel for most students, occurred on Tuesday evenings with all eight students. Advisors warned that fifty percent of students typically repeated the course. My confidence prevailed, as I kept up with the reading, attended every class, and completed all assignments. The members of the cohort grew close because we saw one another daily at work and in class. We preplanned our group class discussions to appear as if we were working through some emotional baggage. Meeting the academic requirements of the program took considerably less time and effort than any of my Cornell University classes.

Halfway through the semester, my grandmother passed. She had been in the hospital for three years in a coma, and I had visited her only twice because she lived in South Carolina. My grandfather had been by her side every single day. No matter how infrequently I saw her, I still loved her. Her death marked the first loss of a grandparent, and I hurt deeply. I left school for a week to attend her funeral.

The first day back in Group Therapy someone brought up the topic of death. It angered me a little since the person knew my grandmother had died recently. I became emotional and struggled to hold back tears. In order to not disturb the group, I excused myself and went to the bathroom to let out the tears I could no longer hold back. I cried for about ten minutes over my grandmother's death. As soon as I could pull myself together, I went back to the group. With regained composure, I continued to participate in what remained of the three-hour class.

The loss of my grandmother was exacerbated by what I interpreted as a rejection by Terry, my friend from high school. We had remained close friends over the years and still spoke of making love one day. He remained unaware that shame had kept me from him. Every time I saw him, I regretted that he could not be my first lover. I had always hoped one day I would be able to look at him and connect to my innocence and share my love from that place. However, when I called to tell him about my grandmother, he broke the news to me that his soon-to-be bride was pregnant with their first child. He had given up on me, and that broke my heart.

CHAPTER 27

J prided myself as the intellect in our group therapy class. I listened well and reflected, as the professor had taught us. I made sure I did not monopolize the group because we were trained to pay close attention to the use of emotional space. I tracked conversations from week to week, hour to hour, and minute to minute so that if someone contradicted a previous thought or feeling, I could address it. When the eight of us joked about which of us would repeat Groups, no one suggested it might be me. Unfortunately, the last night of class the instructor delivered the unwelcome news to me.

Our instructor called students out to the hall one by one while the others who were waiting processed the semester's work. The two people I suspected would not pass had already gone, and they had received a grade of B- or above. Any grade below a B- in the required course would not count toward graduation. I began to assume my cohort would be the first with all students passing but, when I sat in the chair, the instructor told me I earned a C+, high enough to maintain the required GPA but too low to pass Groups.

My heart sank as I offered my sharp verbal disagreement. The instructor recalled my leaving the room when I became uncomfortable talking about my grandmother's death, and interpreted my retreat as an unwillingness to work through the pain. I tried to assure him I understood all of the coursework and had completed the required assignments. I even offered to take a written exam to demonstrate that I knew the content and expectations of group work. After my anxious, tear-filled plea, he looked at me and, in his usual calm, quiet voice stated, "It's as if you are hiding something."

His words triggered an unexpected rage deep within me. Someone or something else arose to protect me. I yelled to drown out his almost whisper, "You don't know shit about me!" For the next sixty seconds, words came out of my mouth that a student should never say to a professor, or to anyone else for that matter, but I was experiencing unadulterated rage. I felt he had looked into a place where I had not invited anyone and he had tried to open a locked door. I felt harmfully invaded and had to protect myself. Whatever had possessed my tongue for those seconds did not understand the irony of trying to convince someone of my readiness to counsel people by cursing them. Wearing my shame on my sleeve, I walked out of the building instead of rejoining the group. I saw no point in continuing if I had to repeat the course.

At this point, repeating the course was the least of my concerns. I felt most irate because the instructor reminded me of the deep shame I had been hiding for three years. To make matters worse, only he taught the course so I would have to face him again. That meant I had to bury the shame deeper, bury the secret deeper.

The next semester, in a class twice the size, those of us who had to repeat Groups lost the support of our cohort. The first night we were asked to go around the circle and talk about how we were feeling in the class where I was one of two Black students. I did not want to fail again, so I spoke my mind. "I hate white people." The African American instructor appeared unfazed. As calmly as he sat when I cussed at him just one month before, he simply asked me to explain myself.

I told him that sitting in a group of white people and being expected to talk made me uncomfortable; four years at Cornell taught me that white people did not give a damn about my life or well-being, particularly not in an academic setting. He invited me to sit with my discomfort, and the students around me to sit with theirs. A petite white woman with short hair and fair skin, about ten years older than me, spoke next. "I hate white people too," she stated. I later learned she had failed Groups in the past too. Her statement profoundly confused and comforted me, as I had never heard a white person say that. I had heard Black people say they hated Black people but never heard a white person say they hated white people.

I became close friends with the woman. She acknowledged the privilege she had experienced as a white person. The room filled with even more discomfort, but the instructor did not waver. For fifteen Tuesdays, the sixteen of us sat around a circle and opened ourselves to pain, confrontation, and discomfort about race, death, relationships, and our fears. We learned about each other and to trust and support one another. I spent my semester undoing some of the psychological damage that racism had caused, but I did not bring up sexual abuse. Twelve months after graduating from Cornell University, I received my Master of Science Degree in Counseling at age twenty-two.

CHAPTER 28

*D*uring my master's program, I began to date a man, Kenneth, two years younger than me. Although only twenty years old, he presented a calm demeanor that made him appear mature. I liked that he grew up in South Hampton instead of inner New York City, as had most of the people I had met. Part of his maturity came from helping his parents care for his two younger siblings. Kenneth's big Howdy Doody smile and bright white teeth made me blush every time he asked me out, even though I said no several times because of his age and undergraduate status. Although we were only two years apart in age, he had completed high school the year I completed my undergraduate degree.

We had been dating a few months when I completed the program. I called my mother to tell her about Kenneth, and that I planned to remain in the upstate NY area to be closer to him. She expressed deep disappointment in my decision because she had waited five years for me to return home and help the family. My father had finally started his church, and they expected me to help it grow. My parents enjoyed showing me off as a parenting success to friends and relatives. I rejected that responsibility and argued with my mother that she sent me to school to make something of myself, not to make something of the family. I assured her she had raised me sufficiently to take care of myself. She admonished me for choosing a relationship with a boy over returning to the family. I longed to tell her the truth, that I hated being home and sharing space with the man who raped my seven-year-old body. I rejected the religious dogma that disempowered people, leaving them helplessly waiting on God instead of taking action to move their lives forward. I resented her subservience to my father and hated the sound of my silence when she fondly mentioned my sister's husband.

The tension between my parents and me lingered when they came for the modest graduation ceremony, which lasted less than ninety minutes, barely long enough to make it worth the five-hour drive. My parents stayed the night in a hotel and headed home the next day. After graduation, they continued to request that I move back home. During phone calls, I could hear my father coaching my mother in the background. She relayed his sentiments as if they were her own and accused me of being ungrateful and disrespectful. She resorted to the ugly words from my childhood, hussy and trifling.

I could not believe she spoke to her most successful child as if I were a failure, referring to Kenneth with equally hurtful insults and insisting I should not chase a boy. I stopped calling home and did not disclose my location or phone number when I moved from Brockport to Rochester. I wrote a letter to Mom once a week so she would not worry about my safety, but never included a return address or phone number. I remained in contact with Bernice but made her promise not to give Mom any information about me.

I moved in with a friend's family in Rochester because I could not afford an apartment. The family had two small children and forbade unknown guests into the house. As Kenneth was home in Long Island for the summer, it gave us a chance to figure out our circumstances when he returned to school. My friend Lisa, whose aunt I lived with, often hung out with me at the house. She was the same age and year as Kenneth and they had met in class at the college. She kept me company while Kenneth and I separated for the summer.

Lisa had lived in Rochester all her life, so she committed to helping me get settled there. I talked to Kenneth only weekly because I was not allowed to use the family's phone to call long distance, and he could not use his family's phone to call long distance without permission. Having Lisa around filled the void. She adored me, sometimes too much and more than I felt I deserved. She bought me gifts and nurtured me. She helped me obtain my driver's permit to find a job, and by the end of the summer I started my career as a drug and alcohol counselor at a community center. I moved out of the family home and into a studio apartment where Kenneth could visit whenever he wanted.

Eventually, I reconciled with my mother. Bernice went to Philly to visit the family, and I would not miss an opportunity to spend time with her, so I visited as well. My mother greeted me with sorrow about my absence. She never apologized for her hurtful words but assured me of her love. I could demand no more from her and continued to visit about one weekend a month. She never again said a negative word about my relationship with Kenneth.

Bernice wanted to meet the young man who had stirred such a controversy in the family, so Kenneth agreed to go with me to Texas to visit her. I told Kenneth he needed to know something before we went and disclosed that her husband once forced me into a sexual relationship. Kenneth became angry, which I later realized came easy for him. I explained that I wanted no trouble, only to visit my sister and feel safe. I asked him to not leave me alone with my brother-in-law, and he protectively assured he would never do so while we were there. He also agreed not to tell my sister our secret.

We traveled to Texas and enjoyed our visit without incident. Kenneth charmed my sister with his big smile and polite manners, and she enjoyed him. Her husband behaved himself and did not approach me. We acted as if nothing had ever happened, but something had happened. There are some things you cannot take back; sexual abuse is one of them. You can deny it, but you cannot take it back.

Relationships are solidified by the secrets people keep for one another. Robin and I shared a secret that maintained the intimacy no matter how much distance existed between us. I hated myself for it. Sometimes survivors do not know the difference between telling a secret and letting it go. Secrets, by their very nature, are kept in the absence of healing. Each time we share a secret instead of living in our truth, we give the secret momentum that offers the violator security. When a violator shares space with a victim without fear of confrontation or reprimand, the silence empowers the violator.

CHAPTER 29

bout a year after Kenneth and I visited Texas, I learned
my most valuable lesson about the difference between
telling a secret and breaking the silence. I thought disclosing the
secret would free me from the fear of exposure and the shame,
and that being in the house with Robin showed my strength. I had
told Kenneth my secret, but I had not broken my silence or let the
secret go. Letting go of a secret breaks the silence to make room
for truth to breathe. Breaking the silence allows natural consequences to occur. Sharing a secret is holding onto the attempt to
control the consequences. As I had not chosen truth, my silence
continued to haunt me.

While visiting my family one weekend, I was caught off guard
by one of my violators. I heard my mother speaking to someone
but could not recognize the other voice. Mom called me to come
downstairs to greet the surprise visitor. I sat up on my bed and
tried to predict the visitor based on the excitement in my mother's
voice. I prepared my mind to see Pam, Terry, or one of my out-of-
town cousins. Instead, when I got to the bottom of the stairs I saw
her chatting cheerfully with her son-in-law. My sister's husband
had made a surprise visit, which had never happened before.

I immediately reacted by mirroring my mother's level of enthusiasm and shortly after, Robin asked if I could ride with him to the store. Of course, Mom agreed, and rushed me to get my shoes on so I could spend time with her only son-in-law. As things had gone well on my last visit to Texas, I naively hoped his intentions were as innocent as he portrayed. They were not.

We drove away from the house, headed in no specific direction. We chit-chatted like platonic friends having a casual reunion. After riding around for twenty minutes, Robin broke a silent pause with an invitation, "Can I take you to a hotel?" The rage I had felt only once before when the instructor suggested I was hiding something arose in me again. I swore at Robin and insisted he take me home. "I am not fucking eighteen years old! I am not in your house! And I am not a virgin! I don't want anything to do with you! Take me home right now, or I swear I will tell my sister!" He did not further his request and immediately turned in the direction of my house. When we arrived, he did not come back inside. I got out of the car and slipped back to my room without being seen by my mother.

Packing and unpacking the pain is the routine of the survivor who is committed to protecting the secret. The victim's guarding of the secret gives perpetrators their power. As long as the victim keeps the secret, the perpetrator controls the victim. I refused Robin but accepted the secret, which cost him nothing. He had nothing to lose and could choose other victims, betray my sister's trust, or try me again at a different time and place. My silence gave him the freedom to do so. On the other hand, I could pretend I did not hate myself, appear perfectly fine, and be the hero of my family. My silence also allowed me the freedom to choose those things, but I paid for it with suicidal ideation that I never disclosed to anyone. I felt more and more distant from myself, as it took an increased effort to hide the shame.

CHAPTER 30

*B*efore long, Kenneth moved in with me. I began home visits with him during his school breaks. His parents required us to sleep in separate rooms. I slept in his bed, and he shared his little brother's room during my stays. Kenneth's mother expressed concern about my interest in her son, given our age difference. She urged me not to distract him from his education since I had already obtained mine. I assured her I prioritized his success above our relationship.

Kenneth became my secret-keeper and we talked about a long-term future together. We did not get engaged but held discussions about marriage. I loved and dated him exclusively, but did not want to live together for long without being married. I wanted to know we were moving in that direction. I did not tell him about the visit from my sister's husband because I felt foolish for getting in the car in the first place. I had not told him about the other violators either. I assumed I would disclose everything at some point before we got married.

I joined a local church and a national sorority to establish social support in my new community. Most of the women in the organization were at least ten years older than me. My time with them focused on boring meetings about fundraising or community service. Other than that, I saw a few of them at the church we attended. One of the sorority sisters had taken me to it as an outing during my pledge period, and I appreciated the positive messages and laid-back atmosphere.

Kenneth taught me how to drive his stick shift car and I became a licensed driver at the age of twenty-three. I had bought a car two weeks earlier to get to my new job in the suburbs, driving a half hour to work. Kenneth drove an hour to school each morning. I could not give him a key to the apartment because his name was not on the lease. Therefore, he would wait for me to get home from work before he returned to the apartment. He did not mind, as he stayed on campus to study most days and liked having most of his schoolwork completed before seeing me. He went to the tutoring center and the library every day after his last class. He found school challenging and spent considerable time on his academics. I sometimes helped him although, the more I helped him, the meaner he seemed to become. He wanted my help yet resented it at the same time.

One morning he left the apartment for school to find that his car had been towed from the spot where he had parked it for months. My attempt to console him escalated into an argument. He never calmed down quickly and I had learned to let him cool off in his own time once he became angry. He blamed me for his car being towed. The argument escalated, and we got in each other's faces with raised voices. I grabbed his shirt with both fists and yelled at him. He pushed me hard, and I fell back onto the couch. I retreated for a few seconds of perplexed silence, then walked past him to the phone. He asked my intention in picking up the phone, and I told him, "to call the police." I explained that he would not get away with putting his hands on me and pushing me around; I would not allow abuse. He apologized and begged me to put the phone down, which I did, but then went to my closet and began to pack a suitcase. I told him that when I returned in two days I wanted him gone. I would allow no one to threaten or harm my body again. I had been through too much and given up too much control and could not live with the threat of harm under my roof.

I had lived too much of my childhood feeling unsafe in my home to live that way as an adult. I would not wait to see if he would fly off the handle and hurt me. His actions toward me were not out of character for him; it was an unveiling of character. I feared being groomed for physical abuse as had happened for sexual abuse and I resented Kenneth in a way that would never go away.

I drove to Buffalo to see my father's sister for the weekend. Aunt Becky disliked my father, so we never talked about him. But she loved her nieces and nephews. She welcomed me to visit her anytime. I told her what had happened, and she let me stay for the weekend while I sorted through my emotions. I admired Aunt Becky. The tall, dark, and beautiful stature ran in my father's family, and Aunt Becky wore it well. I had never spent time alone with her and her two little girls, but they spent time at our home whenever they visited Philly. I made sure to show my appreciation for the stay by requesting to do the dishes. She accepted while she and the girls kept me company in the kitchen.

Aunt Becky told me I could stay as long as I liked, but I returned home two days later. Kenneth had not left because he had nowhere to go, as he had given up his apartment to move in with me. We had both cooled off, and he apologized with great sincerity. I accepted his apology on the surface. I believed he felt sorry, but was unconvinced he would not harm me in the future. We stayed together in the apartment while I mentally planned how to end the relationship over the next few months.

I told Kenneth I needed to move back to Philly at the end of that semester, and he would have to find another place to live. I gave financial reasons for moving rather than addressing my fears about being in a permanent relationship. I loved Kenneth and had mixed feelings about leaving after four years. He asked me not to break up with him when I moved to Philly and I agreed. I wanted to hold on as long as possible.

CHAPTER 31

y life seemed to be a series of making the least damaging choice amid the worst circumstances. I had lived my entire life between a rock and a hard place and feared moving back home to my parents' house. But, I felt ill-equipped to continue in the adult world on my own. I desired to spend time in my mother's bed curled under her while she spoke of how I made her proud.

I asked one of my uncles to bring his truck to help me move. I packed up my belongings and returned to Philly at the age of twenty-five, after leaving home at seventeen. My parents welcomed me. I told them half the truth, that I could not afford to live on my own. I needed time to catch up on my car and school loans and to save money. I chose not to tell them about my fight with Kenneth.

I had too many possessions for my small bedroom at home, so I moved into the messy basement. Clothes were everywhere, along with an assortment of discarded items including broken electronics, cheap tools, old pictures, and dilapidated furniture. Two days of intense cleaning made the space livable. I did my best to help with cleaning the rest of the house as well. I cleaned bathrooms, straightened the living room and washed dishes, but refused to clean my brothers' rooms or wash their clothes. I regularly removed forgotten or discarded clothing from the basement area and returned it to the bedrooms or threw it away based on my interpretation of value. My mother and brothers reprimanded me for discarding items they wanted, but I argued that if they valued their things, they should have taken better care of them.

I returned home with open rebellion, the only way I knew to protect myself. I refused to go to church and participate in my father's religious charade. The first time I attended his church he made disparaging and inappropriate comments about my mother during his sermons. I refused worship under his leadership, much to my mother's displeasure. She continued to pray for him.

I kept to myself and spent little time with relatives. I wanted only to work and save enough money to get an apartment in upstate NY in a year. I would make sure not to allow any man to move in with me ever again. Although I remained in a long-distance relationship with Kenneth, my heart for him had changed. We talked on the phone about twice a week and my parents even allowed him to visit for a weekend and sleep in the basement with me. My sister Gwen fussed about Mom allowing me to have overnight company, a privilege she never granted my older sisters. I felt certain my mother would rather have Kenneth visit me than for me to live six hours away with him.

Gwen had two children now and asked me to serve as godmother to the younger child, Danny. I had no interest in having children of my own, so I welcomed the role as godmother. Moving home gave me time to get to know him and help her out a little.

My mother did not work but spent all her time trying to help my sister with her boys, help my father with the church, and keep up with her sons' lives. She still cooked a big dinner every Sunday and continued to play the lottery for my father every day using the street numbers, even though the legal lottery now existed.

Dad still preferred the street numbers because it paid out more. Mom hated that Dad spent so much money playing numbers but dared not deny his request to make the transactions for him. I enjoyed hanging out with my mother on Saturdays, and we usually went mall shopping.

My father still spent little time at home during the day, despite that he had retired before he started his church. When at home, Dad stayed in his room reading his bible. We missed the family reunion that summer because he did not come home to drive us to South Carolina. When he finally arrived, my parents fought about his delay. She, as always, made excuses for his behavior. I, too, kept my family secrets and embraced the dysfunctional patterns of behavior that maintained them. I twisted reality to survive because I lived in fear of being discovered. I made my pain invisible for my truth to remain unknown.

James generally slept on the living room couch with the television on rather than in his bed. I no longer feared him but hated being around him and never exchanged any unnecessary words with him. He did his thing, and I did mine. However, I could not avoid that damn Christmas gift activity. I hated Christmas shopping with Mom and helping her look for presents for him. I could not explain to my mother that I abhorred buying James anything for Christmas. Instead, I helped pick out socks and t-shirts so we could move on quickly, dying a little inside every time.

CHAPTER 32

A neighbor helped me find a job where she worked as a psychiatric nurse. I worked as a psychiatric technician on the night shift. Although overqualified, I accepted the position because it paid well. The other two technicians on my floor also had master's degrees. We were responsible for monitoring the locked unit of young adults between the ages of eighteen and twenty-four. Two of us worked each night unless a patient was in restraints, as monitoring the environment required two people. A third would be called on duty to watch any patient in restraints.

I also facilitated alcohol education workshops at the naval base for personnel who had received alcohol-related sanctions. I facilitated the one-week-long seminar every six weeks, and went directly to the naval base after my overnight shift at the hospital, which was particularly exhausting. I learned compassion from working with patients who had severe mental health issues, including clinical depression, psychosis, and eating disorders. But working at the naval base subjected me, once again, to the barrage of unwanted advances.

In addition to holding two jobs, I helped my mother care for my godson Danny during the day while my sister worked. My mother drove my sister's older son to school while I watched Danny. When I got home at 7:30 in the morning, I would go to bed. Danny developed a habit of finding me and waking me up. I enjoyed him awakening me with his tiny childish voice and smooth hands. I usually played with him for a few minutes, and occasionally we would fall asleep. Most times I put him on my back to carry him up the steep stairs to care for him until my mother took over.

One morning I got home late due to a dentist appointment. My mother heard me come in the door and asked me about Danny. I told her I had just gotten home, so I had not seen him yet. In a panic, we searched the house top to bottom calling his name. We could not find him inside, so we began to scan the neighborhood. Danny had twice roamed the neighborhood alone until a neighbor observed him and escorted him back to the house, but no neighbor reported seeing him this time. We crossed the big street to look, and after thirty minutes of searching, we decided to call the police before we contacted my sister at work.

We waited anxiously for the police to arrive to take the report and help us. We had searched everywhere we thought Danny might go. With each passing moment, the panic in me became more difficult to control. I felt angry with my mother for not paying attention to him but tried not to blame her. I wished I had come right home after work since I was responsible for watching him during the day.

Just moments before the police arrived, I heard the sound of a tiny voice coming from the basement. Then I heard my name, "Aunt Rose," called with the slightest whimper. I hurried downstairs to find Danny sitting in the middle of my bed, barely visible from the covers. He had apparently fallen asleep under the bundle of covers, the only place we had not looked. We deductively concluded that Danny climbed into the bed looking for me as usual. Not finding me, he must have fallen asleep waiting for me. The basement stairs were scary, and Danny likely chose to wait for me to rescue him rather than to negotiate the stairs alone. He slept through the frantic search. I took my responsibility as godmother and aunt seriously, and the Danny scare shook me.

At work, we had a patient with an intellectual disorder and psychosis. His vocabulary contained fewer than one hundred words, and even those were not articulated clearly. He required assistance to eat and could not follow simple directions. One night all three technicians had to work the floor because the patient was in four-point restraints, as he had smeared his feces all over his room. Since hospital procedure required direct observation of patients in restraints at all times, we took turns sitting by the patient's side for our entire shift, rotating every hour when we did floor rounds.

The restrained patient was very agitated and uncooperative. His frustration caused him to lash out at the technicians who observed him. As all of us were Black, he spent the entire night chanting the word "nigger" at us. Nigger, nigger, nigger, nigger, nigger, nigger, nigger, nigger, nigger, nigger, nigger, nigger, nigger, nigger, nigger, nigger, nigger, nigger, nigger, until he was out of breath. He would catch his breath for a few minutes and then repeat the mantra. He paused, conscientiously, for the white nurse to talk him through his medication routine.

I should have been able to ignore him because of his condition. Someone so low-functioning should not have bothered me. Instead, his use of this ugly word hit me forcefully as I thought, "This patient has a vocabulary fewer than one hundred words, yet, one of those words is reserved for people who look like me." Someone taught him the word "nigger," directly or indirectly. He did not learn it from television, as the media prohibited the use of the word in 1988 because people understood the pain it caused. I doubted the patient had picked it up in any social setting, and assumed he learned it in his home.

An individual who could not teach the patient to use the bathroom without assistance, had modeled the use of language to harm. Someone who could not teach him to ask for a sandwich taught him to insult another person who could teach him. Someone taught him the meaningful value of his skin color compared to mine. The patient flaunted the word as an intentional insult based on the understanding that his life had more value than mine. In spite of his intellectual deficit and a severe psychotic disorder, he believed his circumstance was above being born a "nigger." He was the only patient I ever despised.

The experience spoke volumes about systemic racism in America. It is understood by all, yet denied. This patient smacked me in the face with the truth, the same as the student who wanted Black people to go back to the cornfields when Reagan was elected.

CHAPTER 33

I needed a break from Philly and agreed to meet Kenneth in Rochester for a weekend. We stayed in a cheap motel because, similar to my previous situation, he rented a room in a private home and the owner did not allow overnight guests. He had moved back to Brockport to shorten his commute to school, and two months had passed since we had seen one another. During our weekend together, I had a seizure. When I regained consciousness, I knew I had experienced more than my usual fainting spell. I could feel the seizure happening in my brain. Kenneth confirmed that my eyes rolled and my body convulsed. We went to the emergency room, but the ER physician found no cause for immediate concern. He told me to follow up with my regular doctor when I returned home. I dreaded going home. I processed that living in the house with James triggered the seizure, as my body could not handle the stress of reuniting with its violator.

When I returned to Philly, I went to the doctor as suggested. Medical tests indicated normality of all brain activity. Nevertheless, the doctor saw fit to prescribe a life-long prescription of

Dilantin to control the seizures. I reminded him that I had been free of seizures for 20 years. When I expressed that I had no interest in taking preventive medication, the doctor informed me that I was legally required to accept the drug treatment and, if I refused, he would report me to the Department of Transportation. He emphasized that my driver's license would be revoked immediately.

I complied and began taking the medication, which made me feel out of touch with my surroundings. I had not had a drop of alcohol or weed in years, but these pills gave me a buzz more intense than any I had ever experienced. I felt too disoriented to drive to work. Thus, my mother now had me as a burden. I had to request an extended break at work to get through the night. We usually got an hour to nap during our eight-hour shift. My co-workers kindly afforded me an extra thirty minutes while I adjusted to the medication.

One morning I picked up the newspaper on the table to read an article. I could not comprehend the story in the *Philadelphia Inquirer*, likely written on a sixth-grade reading level. My brain made no sense of the words on the page. I decided to stop the meds after only three weeks. Fortunately, the Pennsylvania doctor had no influence over my New York State driver's license.

Moving out of the house became a priority after the seizure and the doctor's threat. I had relatively little money saved but had caught up on my car payments and school loans. I made a few phone calls to my sorority sisters and asked for their assistance in finding a temporary place. After eleven months in Philly, I moved back to Rochester, New York. A sorority sister allowed me to stay with her while I looked for work. I put the word out among everyone I knew that I needed a job and my boss from graduate school contacted me about an opening for a counselor position. He even agreed to write me a reference, although I feared what he would want in return. I got the job but never spoke with him again, not even to thank him.

I moved to Oswego to work as a therapist. Kenneth officially ended our relationship after two random one-night stands initiated by me. I learned men dislike being used for their bodies, just as women do.

$\mathcal{T}$he new job was well-suited to my experience and education. SUNY Oswego is located along the shores of Lake Ontario, and the counseling center sat on the edge of campus, a stone's throw from the lake. My large office had a private bathroom and a couch, as well as the traditional therapist's chair and desk. I was the fourth therapist on the counseling team, and we addressed all students' nonthreatening mental health issues.

Most students who came for counseling were dealing with relationship issues, stress from school, or roommate problems. They used the fifty-minute session to vent and to seek advice or encouragement to get them through the next seven days or seven weeks. Students sometimes remained the entire hour and left me with no time to complete my notes before the next client. Even with four therapists, the counseling center appointments filled quickly.

We tried to schedule the students with less severe issues two weeks out to fit in the more distressed students and kept a few open appointments for students in crisis. Only once did I have to refer a client for a psychiatric evaluation. She appeared delusional in her description of experiences and not adequately oriented to place and time, and I felt uncomfortable allowing her to leave my office. I asked her to wait for me to find information about one of the topics she addressed while I surreptitiously went to inform the director of my client's mental state. I returned to the client while the director made arrangements for campus safety to transport her to the hospital for psychiatric evaluation. When public safety entered my office, I explained to the client that the officers would take her to the hospital to further evaluate her concerns. The client cooperated and left my office and I never heard from her again.

The handful of Black faculty and staff at the college formed an organization and met monthly for lunch. There were only five Black professionals within my age range and I met them all at the first luncheon I attended. One male, a residence hall director, stood out because he was the best-dressed person in the room even though he had the lowest ranking job. Initially, I made little effort to get to know any of them personally because I traveled back and forth to Rochester for most of my social needs. I attended church, hung out with sorority sisters, and continued to spend time with a few friends from graduate school who lived in Rochester. I worked during the week and usually spent weekends in Rochester.

About three months into the job a student friend, Janet, informed me that I had a campus admirer. She and I spent time together because we were in the same sorority and I assisted her in recruiting new undergraduate members. She described my admirer as a hall director who dressed in suits. I recognized this description and knew exactly who she meant. "He's too damn big for me!" I reacted, and she laughed. Kenneth stood just over six feet and weighed one hundred and ninety pounds, the heaviest man I had ever dated. Ron appeared quite heavier and taller, and the thought of intertwining our bodies intimidated me. I rejected any notion of dating the well-dressed hall director.

Helping Janet with recruiting gave me a reason to spend weekends in Oswego. One Friday evening after a meeting we ran into
the hall director playing the piano, in a suit, in the student union.
We stopped to admire his talent. After he finished he chatted with
us for quite a while. Before I knew it, Janet had left me alone with
him. We continued to talk and he impressed me enough to agree
to hang out with him.

He had finished coursework for his master's degree in
Wisconsin before taking the hall director position. He pursued a
job that would offer him the flexibility to complete his thesis and
earn his degree. Although his schedule was unpredictable due to
student crises, the position offered him the downtime to finish
writing his thesis; and he planned to complete his degree in a few
months. He played noon basketball on campus for fun and invited
me to play with him.

Meanwhile, counseling sessions with students became intense.
A student initially came in to address her engagement to a man
she did not love. However, after several sessions she began to
discuss their depressive sexual relationship. We explored her
previous relationships for comparison, as is required of a
therapist.

The client disclosed that, homeless at the age of fifteen, she
moved in with a thirty-three-year-old kind stranger who took
care of all her needs. In exchange, he required her to have sex with
him whenever he wanted. She perceived this as fair because it
saved her life, although she did not desire to have sex. Between
the ages of fifteen and eighteen when she left to live on her own,
she had three abortions because the kind stranger forbade the use
of birth control. She felt grateful he had paid for each abortion as
she did not want children. However, he offered her no choice in
that decision either, insisting on each abortion and sex without
protection.

No sexual consent campaigns existed in 1989, and Title IX did
not focus on sexual harassment and abuse. No internet existed to

search for information or find support groups. I drew upon my experience with my sister's husband to guide the client without telling her about my victimization. I advised her that no one had the right to require sex for any reason or the right to refuse a partner's use of birth control. We began to explore her decision to marry along with her issues of sexual assault.

A male client also came in for relationship issues but took no time to reveal that his uncle had sexually assaulted him as a child. We worked on issues of anger in order that he could develop healthy relationships. A third older client dealing with childhood sexual abuse sought help to address the issue of her mother's compliance. In the client's youth, her father had repeatedly sexually assaulted her and her sister and the client believed their physically abusive mother knew of it. The client confronted her mother, who responded, "When I was pregnant I promised your father he could do it if the baby was a girl." The mother had sanctioned the sexual abuse of her children. My heart sank from hearing this experience and I shared that I had been raped by my brother when I was seven years old. I knew my disclosure symbolized a deterioration of defenses.

CHAPTER 35

I needed a distraction from work so began spending more time with Ron, the hall director. He talked a lot about education because he wanted to earn his Ph.D. after he completed his master's. His interest in learning captured my attention, as I still found intelligence sexy. His interest in world travel made me see him as a risk-taker, a trait I admired as well. He had twice lived in Denmark and I had never dated anyone who had traveled outside the country, much less lived outside of the country. His interest in travel, seemingly, prevented him from developing long-term relationships.

Ron expressed interest in a committed relationship but I did not yet want to commit. When I asked if he had been careful or lucky in avoiding fatherhood, he replied, "Both," but expressed interest in having children one day. He had three younger sisters, one my age, one older and one younger than me. He was five years older than me and more mature in every way. He watched the news, a sign of adulthood in my mind; I never watched the news. He also read a lot while I cared little for leisure reading since completing my formal education. Earning two degrees by age twenty-two had zapped all of my enthusiasm for reading.

He wined and dined me on dates, not just hung out. He picked me up, took me out and returned me to my home without expectations. I planned a rendezvous for us as well and took my new beau to a Pattie LaBelle concert in Rochester, my old stomping grounds. Pattie LaBelle began her career in Philly where I grew up, so I had particular admiration for her. Her sensual voice and beautiful ballads made you want to fall in love. I felt us heading in that direction.

In order for Ron to travel to Rochester with me, he had to arrange time away with his staff because, as the hall director, he had to be accessible at all times. I picked him up, drove us to Rochester and dropped him off at his apartment, just as he had done for me. I also invited him to church in Rochester where Pastor Garlington taught, not preached to the audience. He ministered that God should be sought within ourselves, not in a building or a clergy member. The pastor discussed personal responsibility as more important than waiting for God to fix our lives. The pastor led us toward love as the answer to most problems and identified fear as the cause of them. He never threatened people with hell or hardship as a consequence of sin, nor took more than one collection during service because he did not believe in begging people for money or requiring a certain amount of money from members. He empowered people rather than taking power away from them with fear. His positive and empowering messages were worth the hour drive from Oswego.

Ron admired me and expressed more interest in my brain than in my body. He reminded me of my Cornell dating days, never requesting anything other than my time and attention. Cautious about getting involved with a colleague, I initially hesitated to offer anything more. I also wanted to be sure I had permanently broken my ties to Kenneth since we had dated so long.

Nonetheless, as my time with Ron increased, I savored his attentiveness, gentlemanly gestures of kindness, and patience in moving forward. He sang to me and played the piano whenever the opportunity presented itself. He held doors open, held my hand, and always departed with the proverbial forehead kiss. He invited me to a Branford Marsalis concert on campus, as jazz was his favorite music genre. I did not inform him that I did not care much for jazz. Instead, I decided to make the evening special and planned to ask him to stay the night with me after the concert.

I sat through the concert filled with anticipation. I had not revealed my intention and Ron was prepared to walk back to his hall when the show ended. As we walked out, I extended my invitation, and he made a quick call to his staff to check in and inform them that he would return in the morning. I lived only ten minutes from campus, making it easy for him to accommodate the spontaneous night away. Back at my apartment, our bodies moved closer and closer until they intertwined. I led; Ron followed. He adjusted for our size differential, and I trusted him. His two hundred and fifty pounds lay comfortably upon me like a blanket on a cold night. He warmed me inside and out and I exhaled into his gentleness. He was my friend; he became my lover.

At the office, session by session, my barriers came down as I counseled clients with histories of childhood sexual assault. I began to feel anxious, and the flashbacks of the stairs and bathroom returned. One night while in my bed I had a vision of my brother-in-law standing by my bedroom door threatening me to remain silent. I could smell and hear him as well, or the presence of him. I froze, wondering if I was going insane. I turned on every light in my apartment.

These visions repeated for weeks. I could not sleep because I feared what felt like hallucinations. My co-workers noticed a difference in me, as I seemed distracted. I disclosed that I had three clients who were triggering my memories of sexual abuse. The boss immediately reassigned my clients and, for the first time in my life, someone referred me to a therapist.

PART III

Most survivors come to the healing path kicking and screaming like the toddler who doesn't want to be pulled off the playground for a diaper change in spite of the bad smell and skin irritation. We come with resistance. We want to feel better by doing the same things, holding the same beliefs, and thinking the same way. We are seeking comfort, not growth. Consequently, reaching the path is different from committing to the journey. Many survivors arrive for the interview but turn down the job. We sit on the side of the pool and dip our toe in the water but never get our suit wet. We go to the dance but never get on the dance floor. Survivors can read about healing, participate in groups, go to therapy, pray for healing, but until we move forward with an intention reinforced by a change that comes from within, we get nowhere. We simply hang around the neighborhood; I circled the block many times.

CHAPTER 36

My therapy consisted of crying profusely and hitting a life-sized doll with a bat to get out my anger. I was an unstable mess and kept waiting for someone to recommend in-patient psychiatric care. I did not feel fit to be in society, between the visions, the suicidal ideation, and the depression. No one could see beyond the suit and the smile. Hitting the doll with the bat did little to bring relief. The therapist missed the fact that I directed most of my anger toward myself. I hated me, so hitting a life-sized doll that represented the violators did not help. I hated my commitment to silence and how small I had become to accommodate the silence.

I wrote to Ron to explain my mental health status and told him that dealing with childhood sexual abuse meant I should not be in a relationship. I dropped the note off at his apartment on my way to work one morning. He contacted me and asked to meet. I could not convince him of the seriousness of my mental deterioration. He continued to reference my beauty and intelligence as if I could not possess those qualities and also be mentally distressed.

When I insisted we should not be lovers, he replied that he did not care about sex. He wanted me and my brain with him. I agreed to continue to see him if he went to therapy with me. He agreed, hesitantly, because we had to break through cultural barriers since our community frowned upon receiving professional help for emotional concerns.

I told my therapist to expect my partner at the next session, which she also had recommended. When we arrived, she initially asked Ron to observe. Shortly into the session, I regressed to my seven-year-old self, balling up on the floor and crying, then angrily hitting the doll with the plastic bat. I could not use words to express what I felt or speak about what had happened in full sentences. I would give only ages, violators' relationship to me, and places: brother, cousin, sister's husband, seven, fourteen, eighteen, couch, basement, bathroom. The remaining speech was jumbled in sobbing and ramblings that could not be understood. If I had been in my childhood church, I would have been considered demon-possessed; I felt possessed.

When the therapist settled me enough to sit calmly, she asked for Ron's input. Bewildered, he indicated he did not recognize the person crying. He described his version of me so the therapist would understand the woman he dated was much stronger. The therapist, in turn, explained to him that "the person who you just witnessed is who you are dating."

Ron came to one more therapy session, but he never understood what the therapist tried to explain. Blinded by love and desire, he refused to accept that I had serious mental health issues in spite of the evidence before his eyes. Instead, he promised he would love me no matter what had happened in the past. He thought he could love me enough to make the post-traumatic stress episodes disappear. I wanted to believe it too.

We continued to date, but awkwardly. The first time I tried to make love to him after the therapy session, I asked him to remove my clothes. He asked if I was sure, and I replied yes. But every way he tried to proceed triggered anxiety in me. He could no longer kiss me because that reminded me of Larry. He could no longer touch my breast because that prompted memories of Robin. A lot of "don't do this" and "don't do that" slowed the process. He patiently tried to follow my commands and reminded me that he did not want to rush sex. He could wait forever to have sex with me. However, if I wanted sex, I would have to allow him to touch me, he teased. I was not sure if I should laugh or cry; I think I did both.

He pampered me every way possible. I did not have a washer or dryer, so he offered to let me do my laundry in his apartment. To save time, I would drop it off at his apartment in the morning, then walk across campus to go to work. I intended to hang out at his place after work and do laundry. To my surprise, the first time I went to his apartment after work he had my clothes washed, dried, and neatly folded on his table. He also had prepared dinner. This became a weekly routine, and I loved the way he cared for me.

Ron, my intellectual, compassionate, well-dressed gentle lover, also enjoyed listening to lectures and going to conferences. The first night I slept at his apartment, I woke up at 7:00 a.m. on a Saturday to an empty bed. I lay there for a while, waiting for him to return, thinking he must have been in the bathroom. I got out of bed to investigate his whereabouts when he did not return. I found him in the kitchen watching a conference video about leadership. It was 7:00 in the morning! What did he need to know about leadership at that time of the day? He always took his responsibility as a mentor and role model for young people seriously. He consistently went above and beyond everyone's expectation. He did it not only for me, but in every facet of his life. I admired his character, yet found him a bit strange.

We played chess, which I had not done since I left Cornell. Kenneth did not know how to play chess. My brother Mitchell had taught my brother David and me how to play, and we had played most Saturday mornings during childhood. Most of the neighborhood children in the projects knew how to play, but when we moved to the suburbs none of the children knew how to play. David hated to lose, and by the time I became a teenager, I would win about fifty percent of the matches. Thus, he stopped playing with me. Besides, he had begun to find girls much more interesting. Ron was also a sore loser at chess, So, we played less often than I would have liked.

I tried my best not to act depressed around Ron, to look and act normal. However, I did not feel emotionally healthy; I felt lost, confused, and traumatized by the pain I once intentionally suppressed. I tried to be the woman he admired, as I wanted to believe that she existed inside of me. I wanted to find her.

CHAPTER 37

The flashbacks lessened in frequency and intensity after two months of therapy, but the anxiety and suicidal ideations remained strong. I felt as though I had jumped into a cold pool of water. Every muscle tensed, waiting for my body to adjust to the temperature. But, my body never adjusted. Neither my body nor my mind felt at ease and I could not shake the feeling of distress.

Death seemed inviting because I thought exposing the shame would kill me. To make matters worse, my therapist went on vacation for two weeks. Surviving week to week without taking my life took diligent intent. Most people wake up wanting to be alive, but every morning I woke, I had to convince myself I should be alive. My therapist's absence annoyed me. Why would someone abandon me in such a vulnerable state? If I had to manage on my own for half a month, I might as well take therapy into my own hands. While my therapist vacationed, I took her suggestion to tell my sister the truth. I had to save myself.

I wrote a two-page disclosure to my sister to tell her I was currently in therapy to deal with sexual abuse. I started out the handwritten letter by advising her to read the message when alone due to its sensitive nature. I told her I had three violators and revealed each and what occurred. I admitted I had no memory of what James did to me, but I believed he raped me. My cousin Larry, who had died the previous year, did not live a good life after he moved out of our house. I told my sister he molested me while he lived there. The letter continued, stating my deep regret about the third person who violated me. "Your husband made me have sex with him." I asked for her forgiveness for waiting so long to tell her. I dropped the letter in the mailbox and waited for the phone to ring days later. I had no idea what to expect, but sending the letter lifted a massive weight off my shoulders. I prepared for whatever response she offered.

Less than one week after I mailed the letter my sister called me. I had considered only two responses. Either she would believe me and I would have to live with the responsibility of breaking up a marriage, or she would not believe me and I would live with the loss of our relationship. I had no idea of the complexity of the conversation that would take place. The discussion caught me entirely off guard. My sister began by assuring me she believed everything I wrote. I burst into tears of relief and apologized for not telling her sooner. She apologized for her husband's bad behavior. Her acceptance initiated a dialogue that would ominously impact the next twenty years of my life. "The reason I believe what you said about my husband is because I know you are telling the truth about James. I was there when he raped you," she disclosed. Her statement left me speechless. My heart dropped to the pit of my stomach like being on a loop-the-loop roller coaster speeding down the tracks. I gasped for air.

She went on to explain that, from upstairs in our bedroom, she heard me fighting with my brother on the couch. She started downstairs to help me until she heard his voice. She quoted him as saying, "Shut up and let me fuck you." Her words opened the profound sadness in me, immediately followed by intense relief. The "loop-the-loop" roller coaster flipped me upside down in the circle. I felt almost faint from trying to process this new information. I tried to reorient myself to space and time as Bernice confirmed my age at the time of the rape. "Yeah, you were seven years old, because I was thirteen."

Holy shit! The visions were real memories. I was seven, Bernice was thirteen, James eighteen. Fearful he would do to her what he was doing to me, she retreated. She never talked to me about the rape because I always seemed OK. After a while, she assumed I just forgot about it. Now, since I was bringing it up, she had no reason to believe I was not telling the truth about her husband. Whatever the highest relief a person can feel, I felt that day. I had let go of the secret and survived. My sister continued to love me, not scold me.

We spent an hour on the phone sorting through the details of the abuse I endured. Bernice wondered if her husband had violated others and apologized for his behavior several times. I kept waiting for her to reveal her next actions toward him. Instead, our discussion ended with a request from her. "Please don't tell, especially Mom." Bernice's husband was just months away from a relocation to Japan, and they had all been looking forward to living in a foreign country. She did not want to disrupt her family life at this time, or for her son to know about his father. I could sense shame from her silent pause when I told her Kenneth had known and my current boyfriend knew as well. She asked me to not disclose further, and I promised I would not.

I accepted the request for silence because I thought I owed her something for believing me, confirming the rape, and restoring my sanity. I owed her for not being mad at me for keeping the secret for nine years. I agreed to hide the truth, ultimately, because I found it easier; but, I did have more to disclose. With the rape confirmed, I wrote my mother a letter to tell her about it. I did not tell her the extent of my memory or mention any other abuse. I wrote to advise her I would not come home anytime soon because I did not want to be in the same home with James.

My mother did not respond to my letter. I called her a week later and asked if she had received it. She confirmed and said she supported me in whatever I needed to do for myself. She did not express outrage, nor shame, nor responsibility, nothing to console me. She merely stated she understood. I expected more, needed more, wanted more than her understanding. I wanted her outrage, at least her apology as Bernice had given. I wanted her assurance that I would not have to see James if I came home. I hoped for her to address the issue; but she did not.

I settled for Bernice's acceptance and my mother's acknowledgment. The flashbacks stopped entirely after my disclosure. My anxiety also decreased, although I continued to decline clients who wanted to address sexual abuse issues. The suicidal ideations, fear of the dark, hypersensitivity, nightmares, fear of abandonment, and shame remained. Fainting spells and other mysterious pain continued, but nothing that a pretty smile, strong vocabulary and Black woman attitude couldn't fix. I was fine.

Ron promised to love me, and did not demand me to change anything about myself. He only expected me to behave as I did in public and not as he witnessed in the therapist's office. With the flashbacks gone, I could do so. His proclamation of love may have been the worst gift he could have given me. I quit therapy just a few weeks later. If I could have someone love me broken, I would not go through the trouble of trying to fix myself. From the day I quit therapy to the day I found myself on the bathroom floor, Ron and I did not talk about the sexual abuse nor my mental health status.

CHAPTER 38

"My momma would like you." As Ron prepared to travel to Wisconsin for his step-father's funeral he kneeled in front of me and told me how much his mother would appreciate meeting me. His tone reflected the sincerity of his feelings. At times he seemed star-struck by me. "I can't believe you are this beautiful and smart and not stuck up." Who was I to argue with infatuation? Instead of continuing to heal, I recaptured my facade of perfection.

Just as I became serious about Ron, he informed me of his plans to return to Wisconsin to be closer to his mother. He had successfully defended his master's thesis and, unbeknown to me, applied for a job at his alma mater. He earned his undergraduate and graduate degrees at the University of Wisconsin–Lacrosse and now accepted a position in the Office of Minority Affairs. He had spent all of his adult life away from home. Like me, he was a first-generation college graduate and the most educated person in his family. His three sisters had chosen traditional family life over professional careers, and lived close to the family home in long-term relationships with their high school sweethearts. Ron's empathy for his mother's loss compelled him to be closer to his family. He also did not want to turn down an opportunity for career advancement.

An internal chain reaction followed when he told me he would leave in two months. Abandonment issues triggered "I am not enough" feelings, and I responded with anger, my "go-to" emotion. I bitterly chided him for lying about loving me and told him I would discontinue the relationship after he left. He tried to persuade me to not judge his love by his decision to support his mother. He needed to demonstrate his commitment to the family and prove himself. He asked me to travel home with him to meet his mother and sisters rather than breaking up with him. His middle sister had a wedding coming up, which would be a perfect opportunity.

His mother and sisters were expecting his girlfriend, but they were not quite expecting me. They mentioned their surprise that he brought home a beautiful Black woman; his previous girl-friends had neither characteristic according to them. They teased me by asking how much he paid me to pretend to be his girl-friend, and teased us for showing so much affection toward one another. They had been with their partners for years, and their undemonstratively affectionate interactions signified their years together. The family appreciated that I knew how to have fun and relax with them.

On our last evening we played Bid Whiz, one of the most competitive card games for Black families, along with Pinochle and Rummy. I partnered with Ron and started off quite well. However, about an hour into being partners, he played a card I thought jeopardized our win. I fussed at him and began a squab-ble. His sisters burst out laughing at us, teasing that all of our lovey-dovey had disappeared at the card table, where we took no prisoners. By the end of the weekend his mother and sister were bantering him not to let me get away and he promised he had no intentions of losing me.

Back on campus Ron and I debriefed the trip. He assured me his mother adored me, as did his sisters. He also shared that he had no intention of ever getting married. He had purposefully remained single at the age of thirty-two. However, he wanted me around more. To my surprise, he asked me to move to Wisconsin with him, not as his wife but as his paramour. To his astonishment, I responded "hell no." I assured him I would move to Wisconsin only as his wife. I loved my job and enjoyed the reasonable commute to Philly. I refused to give that up to move to a state where I knew no one. Moving would put me at his mercy, financially and emotionally. I would never subject myself to that level of vulnerability.

Ron defensively reiterated his lack of interest in marriage. I interjected that I did not propose to marry him but wanted him to know what I would and would not accept to remain in the relationship. He asked if I planned to date anyone once he moved, and I told him I surely would. That displeased him, and he requested me to wait three months for him to get settled in his job, then visit me. He asked for my continued fidelity after he departed. Meanwhile, we had one month left together to solidify our love, and did just that.

Before we separated, I wanted him to meet my parents as well. I invited them to visit for a weekend. My sister who lived at home came with her children as well. My family had tolerated my relationship with Kenneth but never approved of it. They were ecstatic to meet Ron, someone older and more educated. Little did they know their approval of Ron was not as important as Ron's approval of them. I wanted him to meet the people I protected with my silence.

No family could appear healthier than mine. Our routines centered around my mother and the grown-up children looked out for her. After all, she appeared as the matriarch and the martyr. My father served as driver and banker of every outing. I played the perfect daughter, aunt, and godmother. My family never argued or swore at each other and, even as adult children, we never smoked or drank alcohol in their presence. We prayed and worshipped together, served big Sunday dinners, celebrated holidays with extended family, and put gifts under the Christmas tree for unexpected guests.

My mother welcomed everyone into our family. People showed up hungry and she fed them; homeless and she sheltered them; lonely and she comforted them. I admired her caregiving, yet resented the interference with my safety. She forgave everyone for everything and never held a grudge. Mom instilled a sense of responsibility in her girls, while granting independence to her sons. If something went wrong with the boys, my mother communicated disappointment in her sons, such as when they fathered children out of wedlock. However, when the girls made mistakes, she conveyed shame, such as when my sisters became pregnant.

When I refused to attend my father's church because of his hypocrisy, the family admonished me. My mother and brothers commanded me to honor my father, regardless of what he did. No female had a right to judge a man, nor child to criticize their parent. Only God should judge parents, and men judged everything else.

Forcing these male-dominant rules upon children takes away their power, especially females. They may as well hang out a shingle that says, "Violators welcomed here." When a child feels less important than the violator, there is no room to speak. When a parent expects a child to prevent sexual abuse, it is a setup for failure, child failure, which is the reason why many child victims do not speak. When told to be seen and not heard, it is a recipe for sexual abuse, because there is no room to express confusion, betrayal or pain.

My family stayed only for the day and spent a few hours with Ron. I was still disheartened over my mother's response to my letter about James, so I had no desire for them to stay longer. Ron showed them respect and charmed them as much as he had charmed me. If family acceptance indicated our potential for a happy future, we needed to work something out about his pending departure.

CHAPTER 39

*R*on spent his last night at my apartment and we both cried after we made love. I felt too sad to be angry and too angry to be sad. His tears released my pain of abandonment. Although we had committed to three months of trying to work something out, the insecurity of our relationship did not sit well with me. I tried to forget about him by keeping busy at work. On the weekends I drove to Rochester to attend church. I tried to put the sexual abuse behind me, but the suicidal ideations were as present as ever once Ron left. At times I feared driving on the highway, riding with the uncertainty of my will to live.

I wanted to be chosen, to be good enough to be picked, to be loved enough to be selected. I wanted my sister to leave her husband and take care of me, but she did not. I felt as though she blamed me, despite her apology for her husband's behavior. She could not blame him and choose him over me. I knew she held me responsible and pardoned him. She said she did not want her son to know the truth about his father and chose a lie over me. I felt smaller than her lie and less significant than the known violator.

My mother preferred that I walk away from the family rather than remove James from family events. She never asked me a single question about the rape. She could have said so much more to me, but said nothing, which led me to believe she already knew. She did not choose me. She, too, settled for silence and left me with shame.

God had chosen me to remain in this world over Larry, who had died. I did not attend his funeral or offer any condolences; I silently rejoiced. Violators are always violators to their victims, no matter how many years pass. It doesn't matter if violators do good things for other people once they have created such a traumatic experience for the victim. Once an individual is pinned down, threatened, shamed or manipulated beyond their will, and then silenced into a dysfunctional adulthood, there is no greater solace than the death of the violator. Many survivors rejoice in the last breath, as it means God has chosen the survivor.

In spite of not being chosen, I could not stop loving my mother or my sister. They had done so much for me, and their acceptance was what I knew to be love. Love meant birthday phone calls, Christmas gifts, vacations together, the borrowing and lending of money and, of course, keeping secrets. My sister had patiently waited for me to stop wetting the bed and never told anyone or teased me about it. My mother had nursed me through fainting spells and prayed with and for me. My sister had never let me down, and my mother showed her care when I needed her. They had shown me love, and I could not risk losing their love by focusing on my secrets. I should have told them I would rather die than see violators chosen over me. I doubt if that would have mattered, as they fully expected me to take the secrets to my grave.

On the two-lane highway between Oswego and Rochester, the trucks passed my four-cylinder LeMans going eighty miles per hour or faster. I always drove faster than the speed limit, usually around seventy miles per hour. I fantasized as I drove. The slightest twist of the steering wheel to the left would cause a collision and result in my instant death and likely spare the truck driver. I never fantasized about a car collision because I would have put another driver at risk. I had too much compassion for that. Truck after truck, trip after trip, I wondered if my life would end on that road. I could not purposefully turn the wheel left or commit to never turning the wheel. I let fate decide each time I got behind the wheel. Fate favored me, and I am happy it did. Many survivors of childhood sexual abuse are not as lucky.

Childhood sexual abuse (CSA) survivors are at least twice as likely to commit suicide compared to those without such a history. The trauma of CSA is similar to an auto-immune disease of the mind, in which it is difficult to distinguish the good thoughts from the bad. The mind is in a constant battle with itself. For many survivors, the attempt to stop the pain causes more pain, including cutting, abusing drugs and alcohol, binge eating, and starvation. The brain knows only that the parting of the skin, the dulling of brain cells, the stuffing of the belly, the sensation of hunger, or the look of invisibility briefly relieves the pressure. The voices take a nap for a while. The best part of self-harm is the feeling of control, as you can choose things that seem to choose you back, if only for a moment. You say to yourself, "Fuck being chosen," and then you pick your poison. At times, I envied people who could make their pain visible. I understood them, but I could not be them. Fate, (and only fate) did not choose that for me.

CHAPTER 40

I thought Ron had forgotten about me, and I had no way of contacting him once he left me in New York. He told me his plan to move in with a friend until he could find an apartment. He took three weeks to contact me from his friend's house, who had a wife and four children. Finding quiet time to use the phone before bed took that long, according to him. I assumed the truth had more to do with him catching up with old flings and making comparisons. He inquired about my fidelity in his absence.

Jealousy was Ron's most noticeable flaw, swearing that every man on campus wanted to date me. He admitted to an open competition among three of them to see who I would choose. In his mind the contest never ended, though none of the other men had asked me out. I had no interest in any of them, and they presented no threat to Ron's position in my life, although I could not convince him otherwise. I reassured him I had not considered seeing anyone. I did not wait for him deliberately nor look to replace him. I let fate decide; fate chose Ron.

We talked on the phone several times a week once he found a place to live. He wanted to see me and asked that I meet him at a student leadership conference in Indianapolis. He had planned to take a group of students from his campus, so, I made plans to meet him for a three-day weekend.

On our last night after we made love, he noticed a little blood on the sheets and we became alarmed. He asked if I felt OK and I told him I felt no pain. However, apparently, I was not fine because this had never happened before. He showed great concern and suggested I get checked out right away when I got home, then he changed the subject. "Remember when you said you would come to live with me if we were married? Did you mean that?"

I did not answer immediately, and he repeated the question. I answered, "I guess so." He suggested we get married because he wanted me with him; if I needed the security of marriage, he would offer it to me. He never formally proposed. We simply discussed our way into engagement. I had no expectations to negotiate a marriage when he asked me to spend the weekend with him and had been leaning toward saying goodbye. But, committing to him felt right.

We talked for the next hour or so about the feasibility of me leaving my job, our expectations of marriage, and a wedding date. We considered tongue-in-cheek signs that we should get married; both of our mothers had the last name of Jackson. Ron was not a Jackson because his mother had remarried. His step-father and my father shared a surname. Our parents' phone numbers had the last four digits in the exact order, and there were three girls in both families.

Ron and I were members of Black Greek letter organizations, and they were brother-sister organizations. We were first-genera- tion college graduates with master's degrees. We also were both interested in visiting Africa someday. Most of all, we beat the odds of meeting one another by moving to Oswego at the same time. If I had remained in Philly an entire year as I had planned, I would not have gotten the job at Oswego. Ron had taken the Hall

Director position for only one year to make money while he completed his thesis, and had no interest in living on the East Coast.

By now, we had been separated for two months, and he wanted me with him as soon as possible. I suggested we get married on my parents' forty-second wedding anniversary so I would never forget our anniversary, the second day of August. When I returned to Oswego I called my mother to tell her the news. She could have responded with congratulatory remarks or offered motherly warnings about the risk of giving up too much to follow a man. No, she did not respond with either of these maternal gestures. Instead, she complained that Ron had not asked her and my father's permission to marry me. "Nobody asked me if you could get married," she responded.

I thought my mother and I had passed the controlling threshold when I stopped speaking to her after graduation, and that she had resolved to allow me to run my life. After all, at twenty-seven years of age I basically had been on my own for a decade, except the eleven months I had moved back home to break up with Kenneth. I told her my idea for the wedding date, which did not relieve her discontent. Thus, I just asked her to inform my father of my plans and hung up.

I never shared my mother's response with Ron. If I had told him, he would have done as she expected. In the hotel, we had discussed the importance of creating our own rules about marriage and family that would make us happy. I felt comfortable without a traditional proposal and not asking for parental approval. Two independent adults can act as their own agents in the world and do not need permission to spend their lives together. I refused to acquiesce.

I called Pam and told her the news. We talked about marriage for a while, as she had married two years earlier to a handsome and caring Philadelphia police officer. She had chosen me as the maid of honor for her large wedding and was enjoying life with her new husband, except the lack of communication with the ex-wife. Pam wanted to welcome her step-son into their family and home but had great difficulty obtaining consent from the family. Pam's predecessor hid her whereabouts, causing Pam to go through the ex's mother to see the stepson. She considered me smart for choosing a man with no children or ex-wife.

I contacted my only other close friend from high school, the one who had perpetually teased me about my crush on Mr. Metzgar. She fired a series of questions about my soon-to-be husband.

"How did we meet?"

"At work." I replied

"How old is he?"

"Thirty-two."

"How many times has he been married?"

"Never."

"How many children does he have?"

"None." I was certain that surprised her.

"Does he have a college education?"

"Yes, a master's degree."

"Where did he grow up?"

"Wisconsin."

Finally, a pause, and I waited for the next question. No question, just a presumption. "You finally got yourself a white man, didn't you?" She laughed without waiting for my response, asserting all her evidence that I always preferred white men. She started with my relationship with Mr. Metzgar. I laughed with her, but certainly felt no need to defend my racial preference, or her presumption that these qualities could not be found in a Black man. I was glad I did not mention that Ron lived in Denmark for over a year or played golf in high school.

With Ron in Wisconsin and me in New York, we agreed to get married in my hometown of Philadelphia. My father's small church could not accommodate a wedding, and I was happy to not have to consider that option. My mother had begun to split her attendance between my father's church and a neighborhood church. She felt she needed a place of refuge and somewhere she could hear the gospel rather than my father's rants of dissatisfactions from the pulpit.

Mom offered to arrange the wedding to occur at the neighborhood church. We agreed to keep the guest list at seventy-five, then ninety, then one hundred. A service that size would accommodate our budget and her pride, as I was the first girl in the family to have a church wedding. My brother David had a beautiful wedding a few years earlier, but my mother had little involvement in the planning of that ceremony. Since I did not live in Philadelphia, she would have to take care of most of the details. Of course, my godson Danny would be the ring bearer; Pam would be my maid of honor, and my sister Gwen the bridesmaid.

Bernice could not attend because she lived in Japan where the Air Force had stationed her husband. I agreed to preserve the tradition of my father escorting me down the aisle. However, when the clergy would ask "Who giveth this woman to this man?" both my parents and Ron's mother were charged with responding, "We do."

CHAPTER 41

$\mathcal{I}$ wrote Ron at least five letters each week once we were engaged. We had not dated that long, therefore, had plenty to learn about one another before the wedding. Our wedding budget prevented frequent phone calls. Each long-distance call cost anywhere from seven to twenty-seven dollars, depending on the time of day and day of the week, as well as the duration of our conversation. We talked often enough to keep our phone visits brief, but not too often to run up the bill since the letters supplemented the calls.

Ron wrote me once or twice a week and absorbed the bills for most of the phone visits by initiating the calls. We had our first face-to-face visit during Christmas break and I appreciated any reason to spend holidays somewhere other than Philly. His sisters, Viola, Denise, and Jennifer, warmly welcomed me to the family. His mother asked me to call her "Momma" the first time I met her. I appreciated her foresight and expressed my elation that the title would be official.

I saw Ron several times before he arrived for the wedding. When I visited for Christmas, he took me shopping for an engagement ring. We had one sized, and I planned to pick it up on my next visit. During my next visit he gave me the ring and his mother and sisters took me shopping for an off-the-rack wedding dress. We found one that fit my body and budget perfectly. Practical-minded, I moved out of my one-bedroom apartment into a friend's two-bedroom apartment to save money. I did not want to begin marriage with unnecessary debt, especially since we both had hefty school loans.

Ron arrived in Philly two weeks before our wedding date to attend my family reunion and to meet my extended family. We scheduled our wedding one week after the reunion in South Carolina. At the gathering, Ron's jealous tendencies surfaced over males' displays of affection toward me. He could not discern which of them were related to me to determine the level of threat. He requested that I not wear a bikini on our scheduled beach trip. When I confronted him about his jealousy, he lashed out at me and suggested my clothing could provoke the incestuous nature of my relatives.

When I ignored the ridiculousness of his response, he pushed further and blamed me for possible provocation of my past sexual assault. I could not believe my ears. "Are you fucking kidding me?" I wondered, "How did I allow this asshole of a human being into my secret life of pain and sorrow?" He took away from my disclosure that I might be responsible for my sexual abuse? I struggled to find a way for rage and love to co-exist. Stuck between a rock and a hard place, I could tell no one about his comment because I had not disclosed my abuse. Silence prevailed in more ways than one. I did not speak to my fiancé any more than required before our wedding day. I maintained complete silence between us when we were alone and, in public I intentionally directed my comments away from him, even if they were meant for him.

Ron tried to apologize, but I knew he believed what he said. Therefore, his apology meant nothing. I spent the week trying to figure a way out of the wedding. He met every objective requirement for a life partner but miserably failed the subjective test of sensitivity. People congratulated me all week on finding such a good man. The adult me smiled in agreement, while my inner child mourned.

People who believe a survivor can be responsible for their sexual abuse grant safe space for perpetrators to victimize. Those who make insensitive remarks that shame a survivor grant safe space for perpetrators to groom victims. Each time a survivor is required to defend her right to exist without harm, a perpetrator has more opportunity to victimize. Victims do not cause sexual violence, but a culture that induces shame in the survivor perpetuates abuse.

The evening before our wedding I sat alone in the kitchen with my mother. I told her I did not want to marry Ron, I did not love him, I could not love him, and I cried. My mother responded by telling me to go upstairs and try on my dress and make sure I had prepared everything I needed for tomorrow. She said this was not the time to discuss not marrying him, as I had committed to him, and must honor my commitment. I obeyed because marrying a man who believed I might be responsible for my sexual abuse felt safer than talking to anyone else about the pain of my sexual abuse. I shrunk more to fit into my marriage.

CHAPTER 42

*M*y wedding day arrived, and I dismissed all my fears and concerns to promise to love Ron. Eighty-nine family members and friends attended to witness our union; some relatives from South Carolina, and friends from Rochester traveled to celebrate with us, as well as a few close friends from Cornell who lived in New York City. A few co-workers attended from Oswego, including L.C., Ron's best man.

Ron and L.C. met as undergraduates and maintained a close friendship. He had recruited Ron to work at SUNY Oswego, and the three of us spent considerable time together before Ron left. I had sought advice from L.C. to persuade Ron to join me for my appointment with the therapist. L.C. politely intervened in our relationship for that purpose and left the rest for Ron and me to decide. I appreciated him for not continuing to mediate our relationship.

The remaining guests consisted of a host of aunts, uncles, cousins, church members, and a few acquaintances from high school, including Mr. Metzgar. Two of my brothers, David and Mitchell, rolled out the satin aisle runner, and my father escorted me down the aisle to Joe Cocker's rendition of "You Are So Beautiful." Ron and I exchanged vows we had written, promising to bring forth children and raise them in love. We pledged to stay connected to the Black community and to love each other as best we could. We did not promise "til death do we part." The minister asked if I would obey my husband, and I responded, "I will," prompting several people close to me to snicker sarcastically. Danny carried the rings to my husband with the flower girl beside him. Ron anxiously tried to kiss me before Pam pulled back my veil. The congregation snickered again. At 7:30 p.m. I left the Mt. Airy Church of God in Christ as Mrs. Ronald Miller.

Outside the church, I spoke to Mr. Metzgar for the last time. The chat lasted less than a minute because I greeted him in the receiving line with the remaining guests. We had not talked for several years when I sent him the wedding invitation. I smiled when I saw his name on the guest list, though he said he could not stay for the nearby reception. The chauffeur took the scenic route to give our guests time to arrive at the reception. Ron and I partied hard with our guests and headed to the hotel around midnight. My uncle Levi had gifted us with professional limousine service when we asked if he would chauffeur us in his Lincoln Continental. However, the limo service ended with the ride to the reception, so my uncle chauffeured us to our downtown hotel to spend our first night as husband and wife.

We remained in Philly for a week after the wedding opening gifts, packing up, and saying goodbye. We opened all the presents at a post-wedding reception at my parents' house for out-of-town guests. We had requested monetary gifts because we were driving across country with limited space in my compact car, although some people still gave us meaningful keepsakes. Michele, my closest friend from Cornell, gave us a beautiful painting of a wedding scene, with it personalized by the artist. The church board announcement displayed our wedding day, and the names on it read Ronald and Rosenna. The artist's signature appeared discreetly on the bottom of the painting.

We had a cookout at the post-wedding reception, and my mother noted that Ron did most of the grilling, as she was unaccustomed to a man helping out voluntarily. When she saw that I did not fix my new husband a plate of food, she cautioned me to take care of him properly. I assured her Ron did not need me to prepare his dish, and I would do it for him if he directly requested it. He never did, and confirmed his preference to fix his own plate. I saw a look of concern on mom's face that suggested doubt about my ability to keep a husband. Nevertheless, she expressed joy in knowing I had someone to take care of me and she did not have to worry about me as much.

My father gave my husband direct orders to take care of me, informing Ron that I was now his responsibility; I now "belonged" to him. My father verbally relinquished all of his perceived responsibility for my care, as if I had been a transfer of property. He told me if I needed money, clothing, or shelter, I could no longer ask him. I thought to myself, "What kind of sexist showboating bullshit is this?" My father had done very little for me over my twenty-eight years, the first seven of which I did not know him. In the midst of my frustration, Dad said something that pleased me. He told Ron never to raise his hand to me or cheat on me. Dad did not honor the advice personally, but I agreed. My father urged Ron that if he found himself wanting to do either of those things, he should bring me back home. I could always come home, Dad insisted. These words were the most supportive my father had ever said to me and I believed he meant what he said. I loved him for offering me that security.

CHAPTER 43

*R*on and I spent three days driving back to Wisconsin and my reality set in quickly. I left an excellent job with a beautiful view of Lake Ontario from my office to move to a place where I knew no one. We lived four hours from his family and a three-hour flight from mine. Although I avoided going home, I appreciated knowing I could drive to see my family. I had not flown very often, and the distance from my family made me feel isolated.

I loved my new husband but doubted that love deserved the sacrifices I made. I felt I was not as happy as I thought a new bride should feel. The cramped one-bedroom apartment decor still suited a busy bachelor whose fiancé lived a thousand miles away. The king-sized waterbed took up most of the bedroom space. We ate at a small table next to a couch. Just a few feet away sat the thirty-six-inch tube television on a cheaply built plywood entertainment cabinet.

I applied for a job at the counseling center on the same campus where Ron worked in the Office of Minority Affairs. He worried that I might not get the job after I had roughed up the director on the basketball court. I showed no one mercy boxing out under the boards because men allowed me too much leniency as a woman. I would push and shove until the man guarding me made the call for a foul. Usually, he didn't. I would shoot the ball, sometimes from the three-point line, until they decided to guard me closer. The counseling center director took it in jest as I pushed, shoved, and came down with the ball by jumping over his back.

I got the job, but it paid quite a bit less than my previous position, and most students were unenthusiastic about seeing a therapist. My clients in Oswego liked running into me on campus. They held no stigma about seeing a therapist and sometimes waited for their appointment with a friend who happened to be walking the same direction. In my new job, I learned quickly to ignore students if I ran into them on campus, as they did not want anyone to know they were seeing a counselor. Some came to discuss problems as innocuous as roommate dislike and used the counseling sessions as an appeal to break their housing contract since counseling was evidence of distress. Regardless, they wanted their privacy maintained.

We had one television in the apartment and did not like the same shows. We disagreed about what to watch. I hated the news and sports, which Ron watched diligently. He disliked the way I prepared food, finding my taste too bland. He would modify what I cooked, and I felt insulted. He also woke up early, whereas I preferred to sleep late. He drank alcohol, and I had stopped years earlier. He talked excessively when he drank, thus, I complained and asked him to stop drinking. After working as a drug and alcohol counselor for three years, I loathed being around people drinking. However, he continued to drink beer while watching football at home.

Ron knew we had not gotten off to a good start too, but he rarely complained about anything; I complained about everything. We had talked about the big stuff before we married but had ignored the little things we did not realize would make living together challenging. I could not help but think I made a mistake by marrying this man, or perhaps any man.

About five weeks into the marriage I told my husband we needed to have a serious talk. I told him I felt unneeded. He had a full life that he enjoyed. He cooked and cleaned for himself since he did not like the way I did it. He never complained or asked me to do it differently; he just did it himself. When I asked what he needed me for, he verbally gut-punched me. "Nothing," he replied. I held back tears as he spoke. "I'm thirty-three, and I have been on my own since I was eighteen years old. So, I did not marry you to take care of me." He clarified that he married me because he adored me and he wanted me to spend my life with him. He wanted me to be the mother of his children. That all made sense, however, I did not know how to trust that someone would want just to be with me, without needing or demanding anything. That version of love surpassed my understanding.

When we talked about marriage and wrote our vows, I agreed to have two children, but that no longer felt right. I told Ron I wanted to go to the doctor to get birth control pills, as I had not taken them for several months because we discussed having children right away. I now believed that marriage should be more stable before adding children, and he agreed. We both knew the reneging went deeper than delaying children. I accepted it as the first step in our silent resolve to end our marriage after only one month. I had given up too much and had received too little in return. In the back of my mind I wondered how long it would take for me to buy a plane ticket to go home. We had started off our marriage financially broke, so I figured it would take a month. I would just bide my time until then.

Meanwhile, I made my appointment to see the doctor the following week. After making the appointment, I thought about the date of my last period, as I would need that information for the doctor. I quickly recalled the date because I had my period on our wedding day; no bride ever forgets that curse. It had begun three days prior and ended the morning after the wedding.

I realized I had not had a menstrual cycle since I arrived in Wisconsin. My cycle was never late, with the exception of the pregnancy scare in college. While my new husband and I sat on the couch watching TV, I blurted out of the blue, "I'm pregnant." He turned his head toward me and responded with disbelief, which resulted in us going to the store to buy a pregnancy test. We returned an hour later and I peed on the stick, and showed him the positive results.

CHAPTER 44

$\mathcal{I}$ never really wanted children or trusted that I could be selfless enough to be a good mother. I feared a life of sacrifice like my mother. I had regretted the negotiation of motherhood in that hotel room. However, when I realized I had a life inside me, all my hope for humanity came alive. I felt a sense of value for everything; I became alive. Ron and I had made a baby together, elevating him to the most lovable man on the planet. I would have to rise to the occasion by being a good mother and a good wife for the beautiful life I carried inside me.

The pregnancy did not begin well. Nine days after the stick confirmation, a driver rear-ended me at a stop light. I went to the emergency room to check on the baby, even though I felt fine. The tiny size of the embryo prevented any imaging, so the doctor checked for vaginal bleeding to indicate a possible miscarriage. Everything appeared healthy, and I went right home. Fifteen weeks into gestation I woke up with pains in my belly. Ron took me to the hospital, and by the time we arrived, the pain had caused me to wince and whine in the fetal position. My doctor, an intern, came in and performed a vaginal check and found nothing wrong. She called in the OB-GYN specialist, and in the hour that it took the specialist to arrive, three male interns examined me. None could offer pain relief until they could determine its cause. The pain made me agreeable but, in my better mind, I would have rejected three interns prodding my vagina with their fingers. I was angry with myself and with them even as I allowed it to happen. I had intentionally chosen a female doctor because I doubted men to be impartial with my body. I mistrusted male doctors to handle the most sensitive aspect of my body.

When the specialist arrived, he quickly examined me and offered a diagnosis: fibroids. I had been diagnosed with fibroids when I visited a doctor after the bleeding in the hotel room. However, I had no idea that it would interfere with pregnancy. The ultrasound revealed that I had one the size of a pea and another the size of a nickel. At fifteen weeks, they were about the same size as the embryo and fighting over my blood supply. The doctor assured me the baby would win the fight, but it would take another ten days for that to happen. He admitted me to the hospital to monitor my pain while the baby fought for its life, and prescribed Demerol to help me survive the painful battle for blood. I received Demerol through an IV and was required to stay in the hospital until the pain subsided enough for me to take medication by mouth.

My husband felt bad for me and would not leave me alone in the hospital. I could see the feeling of helplessness in his eyes as he watched me in excruciating pain. Two days passed before the pain subsided enough for me to stop groaning and holding my still-flat belly. At that point, Ron went back to work during the day and returned to the hospital when he got off. I finally slept through the third night.

Unfortunately, sleeping through the night caused me to miss a dose of my medication, and I woke in severe pain again. I reverted to the groaning and belly holding. The nurses allowed my husband to sleep in the vacant bed in my room. He responded to my groaning and called the nurse immediately. Suffering in pain the entire day, I told the nurse I needed a consistent dose of medication to manage it and requested that someone administer the medication during the night if I was asleep. The nurses refused and responded with suspicion of drug addiction. If it had happened today, I would have set the alarm on my cell phone every two hours. Instead, I requested my doctor write an order for the consistent administering of pain medicine.

Meanwhile, my concerned husband informed my mother about my condition and she called me. She did not like the way I sounded on the phone. On day seven, she arrived at my bedside with a look of helplessness in her eyes that saddened me. When my intern doctor came in, my mother spoke with her and asked how much longer I would be able to survive in such agony. The doctor empathized with my mother's sadness at seeing her daughter in such pain. I listened in as the doctor explained my dilemma of carrying a child and enduring such discomfort. I could not feel the baby, only the pain of the fibroids. The doctor informed my mother I could decide to stop the pain by terminating the pregnancy, but no one could make that decision for me.

Responding to the concern on my husband's and mother's faces, and the observable pain in my body, the doctor called the specialist back for a consultation. Professional but stern, he chastised all of us for not adhering to his words. "I told you this would take up to ten days. It's only been eight days." He said nothing else and showed no further concern. We had to wait two more days before he would make any further assessment. That night, with my husband beside me, I confessed that I did not think I could tolerate two more days in misery. He agreed to support me in terminating the pregnancy if the pain did not subside by morning.

The morning came and the pain had subsided, almost completely gone. I could sit up, move, and talk freely. I told Ron how much better I felt and he called my mother, who slept alone in our tiny apartment. He picked her up so she could spend the day with me, as he had done for the last two days. Of course, she told us she had been praying, as always, because she lived by faith. My doctor felt almost as much relief in taking me off the IV. I had to remain in the hospital another day to make sure the oral medication managed the residual pain. The specialist came back in with his "I told you so" attitude. After ten days I left the hospital with my husband, happy to return to our bed.

I had lost a few pounds in the hospital, so I took my prenatal vitamins and tried to eat as much as possible. I craved Burger King bacon cheeseburgers, with the pickles of course, but had little appetite otherwise and still relied on pain medication. My mother stayed with us for a week after I came home. I feel certain she would have stayed longer if she had a bed to sleep in rather than a couch. She always showed up when I needed her, or at least when I could express my need to her. I went back to work after being out for three weeks, however, the pain returned after two days. Concerned that the pain would cause me to miscarry, my doctor put me on twenty hours of bed rest at twenty weeks of gestation. I was allowed out of bed twice a day for two-hour-periods.

My husband tried everything to lift my mood, and took me out of the house when I felt well enough. He pampered me with flowers, by doing chores, cooking, and anything I asked. I stayed on an emotional roller coaster, as being home alone and bored during the day made me miserable. I became depressed and cried often. My doctor offered me anti-depressants, but I refused to subject the baby to any more drugs. The doctor, my husband, and I celebrated twenty-six weeks of gestation because a premature baby could survive outside of the womb at that stage of development. Still, the doctor required me to remain on bed rest until thirty-five weeks to give the baby the best chance of survival.

Ron and I began to think about names. In the nineties doctors did not routinely tell mothers the sex of their child but, judging by the slower heart rate and lower belly rise, we guessed that our baby was a boy. We desired that our children have African names to honor our African heritage. We picked out the name Sentwali Gelani for our son, meaning "brave" and "mighty" in Swahili. Since our son had survived such a tumultuous start in the womb, we knew he would be brave and mighty.

We hoped to visit to Africa someday to connect with our lost heritage, often reading books by Maulana Karenga, Amos Wilson, Cheikh Anta Diop, and other Africa historians who attempted to restore the conscious connections between Africa and African Americans. We believed that we could not have Black power without Black consciousness, and we could not have Black consciousness without connection to Africa, the birthplace of all consciousness and the global home for Black people all over the world.

We did not want our child to have the only African name in the family. We decided to change our last name to "Bakari," which means "noble promise," enabling our child to have a full African name: Sentwali Gelani Bakari. Ron applied for a legal change of his last and middle names and kept his first name to honor his mother. He changed his middle name to Sentwali in order to share the name with our presumed son, a daring hunch.

Because we had convinced ourselves that we were having a boy, Ron completed the application for a legal name change. Ironically, Ron's court date for his name change was after my due date. I gave birth to Sentwali Gelani Bakari on May 2, precisely nine months after I became Mrs. Rosenna Jackson Miller. After Ron's legal name change, one month later, I dropped the Jackson and Miller and began using the name Rosenna Bakari. From that day, I referred to my husband as Sentwali, and he used his first name primarily for legal purposes.

CHAPTER 45

A tremendous help, my mother returned to be with me after I gave birth, but did not take over as some grandmothers do. She did whatever I asked of her and doted on me, not just her grandson. She included my husband in everything and commended him for how much he contributed. He cooked, cleaned, changed diapers, and pampered me as well.

I discovered a hernia in our otherwise healthy son at two weeks old while changing his diaper. He underwent surgery to have it removed only six weeks after birth. I bemoaned the level of negative impact on my child. Between the minor car accident, the fibroids and now the hernia, I hoped he would not have to fight his entire life. Baby Gelani became my refuge, and I loved him more than I knew I could love anyone or anything. For the first time in a long while, I felt committed to being in the world. Nothing mattered more than caring for this little human who came out of me.

With "For Once in My Life" by Stevie Wonder playing on the record player, I danced around the house with Gelani in my arms. No matter what happened, this boy would love me, and I would love him. He would need me and I would need him. I had no idea that having a baby would make me so happy, but it did. Caring for an infant required all of me, and I adored him for it. I valued not having time to think and treasured having a focus. I could have ten more babies, if just to hold onto this experience of significance.

We spent our first Christmas with Sentwali's family in Milwaukee. His middle sister, Denise, had a baby just six months older than Gelani. There was plenty of diaper changes, lap holding, and baby talk. Christmas Day focused on the older children since the babies would not remember. Denise had two school-age boys, and Sentwali's oldest sister had a teenager. His youngest sister Jennifer had no children.

After all the presents were opened, Jennifer requested our attention to present the last gift to the family. She held nothing in her hand, so I expected her to leave the room to get whatever she wanted to give us. She did not move and, instead, announced we would have another niece or nephew the following August. She had learned the news only a few days before Christmas. We celebrated her pregnancy all Christmas Day, raising the vibration of the baby talk. Gelani would not get to be the youngest grandchild for long.

My baby had been fussy that weekend, so I did not set an impressive example for motherhood. He seemed continuously hungry and though I increased breastfeeding, he did not respond well. I worried that something might be wrong with my milk. I got a thrush infection after nursing him the first two months, so I feared something else might be wrong. Nevertheless, Jennifer and I talked about all the benefits of breastfeeding, the value of cloth diapers, baby names, and everything else. I felt excited to add another baby to the family and wanted our son to have cousins for playmates.

On the drive home Gelani started crying, and I took him out of his car seat to nurse him. As I positioned his mouth to suckle my breast, he turned away. His tiny hand started to push on my flesh with frustration. I could tell when he started fussing that milk was not coming out of my breast. My mind did a brain scan for the reason no milk would come from my breast, and I had a revelation. I looked at my husband and repeated words of deja vu, "I'm pregnant." He looked over at me with the same disbelief as a year ago. "You're just saying that because you spent too much time with Jennifer this weekend."

I explained to him what the doctor had warned me about breastfeeding when I mentioned to her that we wanted a second child. She cautioned me to not have another baby until I stopped breastfeeding, as pregnancy likely would interfere with lactation. Her information competed with the myth I chose to believe, that I would not get pregnant while breastfeeding. Sentwali and I did not plan for another baby so soon, but had been inconsistent with birth control, which we sarcastically refer to as the "hope method" of prevention: knowingly using birth control ineffectively and hoping not to get pregnant.

Fifteen months after I gave birth to Gelani, we revisited the delivery room to bring his sister into the world, Nailah Iesha Bakari. We did with her as we had done only a year ago with our son. As soon as she exited the womb, the doctor handed her to her father to whisper her name and its meaning in her ear, and give her a message of love, before placing her in my arms. Nailah means "one who succeeds," and Iesha means "life;" she would be one who succeeds in life.

My pregnancy with Nailah had gone much smoother, with no complications. By the time Gelani began to crawl, we had moved out of our tiny apartment and into a house close to the campus where Sentwali worked. He often came home for lunch to check on the children and me. The house had plenty of room for my mother to visit after Nailah's birth. She visited for three weeks to help out and cautioned me against becoming a baby factory. I concurred. By then the challenges of parenting acted as a deterrent.

Gelani learned to say "no" and used the word generously, especially when asked if he wanted to use the toilet. Potty-training a child while pregnant with another had curbed any potential interest in a third one. Gelani also tended to scurry away from me in public. My daughter, on the other hand, wanted to be in my arms all the time and cried if I moved five feet away from her. She would not allow anyone else to hold her. I had my hands full trying to nurse Nailah and potty-train Gelani. Still, joy prevailed.

My mother expected to help out more, but the children rejected her attempts to assist. My son craved independence, and my daughter wanted only me. That left Mom with the mundane chores of cleaning and preparing food, which she did not mind, but wanted more time caring for the children. I could sense that she respected me as a mother and admired the family life Sentwali and I had built. It did not resemble her experience with my father. She expressed pride in having such a dignified son-in-law. Because she could not spoil our children, she spoiled Sentwali. He never lifted a finger to do anything while she visited.

My best friend from high school, Pam, asked about my plans to return to work. She had one child about a year older than Gelani and did not want any more of her own. She had finally worked out an arrangement to spend time with her step-son. However, she would not give up her career. She advised me not to rely on parenting for all of my fulfillment, although I did. If she had only realized how difficult it had been for me to remain connected to this world before I had children, she would have understood. No one understood.

CHAPTER 46

I was not yet aware I was pregnant with Nailah when my brother David called to tell me the doctor had diagnosed him with lupus. We talked for an hour about the diagnosis. He had not spoken to our mom about it so as not to worry her. As we were disclosing secrets, it could have been perfect timing to talk about my sexual abuse; but I feared his judgment and discussed only his concerns. Many people lived long lives with lupus. However, the treatments were less effective for males. The doctors said they could treat his symptoms with the steroid Prednisone, but no cure existed for the disease. They made clear to David that the long-term use of steroids would shorten his life; it would be his responsibility to convey his level of tolerance for quality versus quantity of life.

David had gone to the doctor after sleeping for a day and a half, from late Friday night until Sunday afternoon. His wife Michelle tried to wake him but he kept falling asleep. When he finally awoke, he felt achy and still tired. His doctor previously treated him for alopecia, hair loss. He wondered if he had been misdiagnosed and visited the doctor with increasing concern about his health.

Through bloodwork, the doctor diagnosed him with lupus, an auto-immune disease. I barely understood the meaning of "auto-immune" when David shared his health status with me. My limited knowledge of the immune system included the awareness that it determined one's vulnerability to disease and illness. I knew HIV compromised the immune system and colds could advance to pneumonia and cause death. I knew of no other types of auto-immune diseases. My most significant health concern was getting rid of my baby fat.

An auto-immune disease such as lupus causes the body to poorly distinguish between healthy cells and bad cells. It erroneously fights the good cells and compromises the functioning of the organs, in this case, primarily the kidneys. The doctor warned David that many patients end up on dialysis, and he should think ahead about acquiring a kidney donor.

By the time Nailah arrived, David could not work and received disability income due to the progression of the disease. He could not hide the disease from our mother for long, as one of his legs stiffened, and he had to walk with a cane. David possessed a handsomeness that made him look cool sporting a cane. He eventually needed dialysis and moved back in with my mother so she could help care for him. Before he stopped working he and his wife had separated over irreconcilable differences, though they remained friends. His wife continued to attend family functions and stopped by the house occasionally to check on him. Several friends as well as relatives frequently checked on him.

David's positive attitude overshadowed his physical limitations and his cheerful disposition raised everyone's spirit. No one expressed more gratitude than David and being around him made us feel humble. All the siblings did blood work to see if we could donate a kidney. Three of us shared the same blood type, but I had the healthiest body, making me the best candidate. We waited for the doctor to agree to the transplant, however, David's health deteriorated enough that an organ transplant likely would fail.

In order to receive long-term disability, David was not allowed to have a large sum of money. So, he gave me his savings, ten thousand dollars, which I put away for emergencies. He brought me a check when he came to visit, when Nailah was five months old. Like my mother, he tried to get close to Nailah, but she resisted. She still nursed every two hours and strongly objected to any separation from me, and I rarely left her side. She slept in bed with Sentwali and me, even though her crib sat at the end of our bed. We could not let her cry because our son slept in the room ten feet away, and at least having her beside me made night nursing easier.

During David's visit I decided to take a chance on leaving my husband with the children for the first time. I nursed Nailah and left the house immediately to take full advantage of the two-hour interval, ignoring her whining as I departed with my husband trying to comfort her. I arrived back home two hours later to find my brother rocking Nailah as she cried. I asked if she had stopped crying at all, and they said, "No" in unison. I chose not to leave her again for a long time; my freedom did not justify her pain.

We once took our son to Milwaukee to stay with Sentwali's family for four days so we could drive sixteen hours to a conference to hear Dr. Maulana Karenga and Dr. Naim Akbar speak. We took Nailah with us because I could not leave her with anyone. I nursed her for fourteen months, in spite of her first teeth gnawing my nipples sore at five months old. She never took a bottle or pacifier or sucked her thumb as had my son, but she tried to mimic everything else he did. Thus, she walked at seven months, potty-trained herself at a year, and began talking early as well.

My son enjoyed playing with David, though David spent much of his time helping with home improvements and repairs because I did not have a handy husband. Luckily, I had handy brothers. David's disability may have slowed him, but it definitely did not stop him. He saved us money by upgrading our electrical panel and renovating our attic space into a functional closet and office.

My husband, always appreciative but not helpful beyond paying for the materials, provided good music and conversation while David worked. I stayed busy caring for the children.

David's health saddened me, yet I admired his strength. He kept busy all the time, only at a much slower pace. He often moved about without his cane and had to search for it when he needed it. I struggled to keep the cane away from my son, as he loved to play with any stick. David helped me feed Gelani and put him down for his afternoon nap. David also read to Gelani, watched Sesame Street, and wound up his baby swing. I enjoyed having my brother around and missed him when he left after three weeks.

CHAPTER 47

$\mathcal{L}$ ess than a year after David's visit I received a phone call from my mother telling me David was in the hospital's ICU due to a lupus flare-up. The doctors told my parents to prepare for a funeral, as they believed David would not come out of the coma. He had fluid around his brain and heart, a staph infection, and none of his organs functioned adequately. My siblings and my mother had been taking turns staying with him at the hospital, and he had been in a coma for a day when my family called me. I packed my black dress and children's things and took the first flight out to Philadelphia. My husband stayed behind to work, assuming a funeral would be at least a week away depending on how long David lived.

Bernice had returned to the United States and moved to New Mexico where her husband was stationed after Japan. She and I arrived in Philly the same day and went to the hospital to relieve my mother. We both restrained ourselves from pity. We sat in hope and prayer and beckoned David's heart to stay with us a little longer. Bernice and I strolled down memory lane on the chance that David could hear us. We massaged his arms and his legs and stayed until our mother returned to spend the night with him. I could not stay all night away from my children. I would relieve her in the morning after feeding them breakfast.

Miraculously, David came out of the coma after three days, and we rejoiced. However, the fluid around the brain made him delirious, and his organ function had not improved. He did not recognize me; when I told him I was his sister Rose, he did not believe me. He insisted his sister lived in Wisconsin, which meant I could not be in Philadelphia. At least he had a grip on reality enough to know he had a sister named Rose and where she lived. I told him a list of facts about the times he and I spent together, but he would not budge in his delusion. I tried to feed him, but he refused to eat, and even thought he was outside because a picture of a window faced his bed.

The next day, David's symptoms worsened and the nurses put him in hand restraints during the night because he became agitated and tried to pull out his needles and tubes. Seeing him so helpless made my heart break, although Bernice and I couldn't help but laugh at him trying to convince us to help him escape. "Torque it," he repeatedly exclaimed, followed by some gibberish. Bernice and I probably laughed to keep from crying. The feeling of vulnerability from watching a loved one in pain weighed heavily on my heart. We sat with him, hoping for another miracle.

After sitting with David for a few hours, the nurse called us out of the room to give us information she did not want David to hear. We prepared for bad news. Instead, she told us that someone named "Michele" was on the phone and wanted to know if she could visit with him. His health status required that all visitors be approved by the family and the nurse asked for our consent. We responded that we did not want David to become further agitated by the presence of his ex-wife, but then wondered if we had done the right thing. We decided to take a chance and ask David, as his delusions had subsided and he recognized us. Maybe he would want to see Michele. We asked, "David, do you remember Michele?" His eyes watered with sadness. "Yes, I know who Michele is," he responded quietly. We told him she wanted to visit and asked if he would mind. "That would be great," he replied.

We asked to use the phone at the nurse's station because intensive care patients had no phones in their rooms. We called Michele and invited her to visit, warning her about the severity of her ex-husband's condition. My brother George arrived while Bernice and I waited for Michele. When Michele arrived later George, Bernice, and I remained in the room to make sure her presence did not trouble David. She approached him sweet and kind, and David, as usual, reacted with equal kindness. My siblings and I decided to leave her alone with him while we went to eat. We asked the nurse to keep a close eye on him just in case.

We returned to the room about thirty minutes later to a big surprise. We saw David sitting up on the bed with Michele stroking his hair while he ate without restraints. This patient was not the same person who kept telling us to "torque it." Delusions, hallucinations, misperceptions, and agitations were absent; no evidence of brain glitches remained.

Michele assumed we had merely exaggerated David's condition and asked the nurse to remove the restraints. My siblings and I laughed among ourselves. Married or not, the magic of love still bound them together, and we could not thank her enough. She nursed David back to health for the next couple of weeks until the doctors released him from the hospital. Then she distanced herself from his life again.

I had to take breaks from helping to care for David to love on my babies who waited patiently for my attention. I liked that they had an opportunity to be with extended family, and my mother enjoyed having them around. She remarked that she had never seen children who asked for so little, even at their tender ages. They were content and self-sufficient for the most part. Nailah finally adapted to my not being by her side every second, although she clung to me whenever she could. I needed to love and protect them. Nothing in my past seemed significant, not even the abuse. As long as James was not near my children, I felt fine. Nothing could shake me anymore.

CHAPTER 48

hen I returned to Wisconsin, I picked up the book, "The Courage to Heal," written by Ellen Bass and Laura Davis for, indeed, I had found my courage. Although the book affirmed my right to all of my emotions, it did not lead me anywhere. I did not know what I needed, but I it was not in that book. I read another book, "In the Company of My Sisters," a Black feminist book about self-esteem by Julia Boyd. Maybe I needed to work on my self-esteem, I thought. I did not find my Blackness in it though.

The book spoke loudly about Black women's right to sexual expression as casual sex. I thought about my one-year-old daughter and did not want her right to sexual expression emphasized as having meaningless sex. The author ignored the sexualization of the female slave, whose sexual prowess had never been disputed. Instead, the Black woman's right to abstention had been denied. I wanted my daughter to understand her right to say no to any and all offerings of sex and still feel like a beautiful woman. I desired that she view her vagina as a sacred space where she should invite only people who appreciated and valued her choice to summon them there. I wanted her to understand her right to bodily autonomy, and not to offer intimacy in exchange for attention, as an apology, or for protection, and never out of fear.

Too few books spoke to Black daughters about our history and their rights. I worried that Nailah would not know what to fight for and why we needed to fight for it. I decided to write a book on Black women and self-esteem in case I would not live to see my daughter become a woman; I wanted her to know how I felt about her being a Black woman in a world that would deny her so much.

In 1994, I wrote and self-published my first book, "Self-Love, Developing and Maintaining Self-Esteem for The Black Woman." I went on a few speaking tours but focused on raising our children and homeschooling them. The book is now out of print, but I still have about twenty copies left and read it every few years. I now realize all women need to come to the same understanding of bodily autonomy in the face of objectification, hyper sexuality, and the epidemic of sexual abuse. However, it would be many more years before I forwarded that message. I remained on the speaking circuit for two years before we left Wisconsin for Sentwali to pursue doctoral work at the University of Northern Colorado.

During our pre-marital hotel talk, Sentwali emphasized his interest in earning a doctorate. After we got married, each year life changes made continuing his education less convenient. Two babies, buying a home and David's illness captured all our focus. Nevertheless, when Sentwali received the acceptance letter from the University of Northern Colorado and asked how I felt about it, I agreed to support him.

I preferred moving to Colorado over him traveling an hour to work on the degree at the closest program in Wisconsin. After I agreed, he mentioned he had not received any financial support, suggesting a willingness to delay his acceptance. Well, once I said yes, I refused to back down. It had taken five years for that yes to come out of my mouth and I told him we would find a way.

When we got married, Sentwali agreed to let me handle the finances. I had the task of clearing up our debt and building savings. He put every single penny he earned in my hands. He gave me his check, and I gave him an allowance. At my bachelorette party, one of the married women advised me that I had to do one of two things to have a successful marriage: control my husband's time or control my husband's money. I made sure not to do both, so I managed his money. That came with a lot of responsibility because we had limited funds on one income. I had managed to negotiate a "for sale by owner" purchase of our house after only six months into the marriage, and now had to figure out how to pay for his education.

After some time in the library reading books about money while the children browsed the toddler room, I presented Sentwali with a plan. We would rent the house for two hundred dollars a month profit and take out a six-thousand-dollar equity loan on it as well. We had another six thousand in the bank, and the school agreed to fund four thousand dollars toward his degree if he committed to returning when he completed it. That would get us there and settled until we could both find jobs. We took out education loans to pay for his tuition and agreed to live without medical coverage. Looking back, we accepted a pretty risky plan, but we went for it.

In Greeley, we rented a two-bedroom on the second floor of an apartment complex. We were cramped. We frequented a small playground on the apartment grounds. We homeschooled and loved it. I refused to put my babies in the hands of a stranger for hours each day, as I had seen too much of what public education produced that I snubbed. I did not want my children to go to college as unprepared as I had. I wanted them to be challenged and supported. I nurtured them to be thinkers, not followers. I did not want to expose them to the factory model education system. Instead, we went out exploring every day with the world as our university.

We spent time with diverse people, different ages, races, and economic levels. We explored the parks, mountains, banks, museums, church, stores, car wash and campus offices, as well as people's homes. Below us lived Ms. Bernie, an older woman confined to a wheelchair. She cared for two preschool girls, sisters. We became well acquainted, and she would occasionally watch my children. The sisters sometimes would spend time in my apartment. Ms. Bernie's help allowed me to find a part-time job at the community college, where I worked ten hours a week as a student advisor to pay our utility bill.

As Sentwali completed his first year of school, Bernice asked me to visit her in New Mexico to attend her son Ryan's graduation from college. I wanted to be there for him because none of the other family members could attend. I packed up the children for our road trip from Greeley to Albuquerque in my husband's old Mazda. I looked forward to doing something independent from Sentwali for a change. I had taken my share of road trips alone when I lived on the East Coast and traveled back and forth from New York to Philly. After getting married, Sentwali did all the driving.

I looked forward to the trip alone with the children in the car until I got to Raton Pass, which was about halfway. The incline to over seventy-eight hundred feet was steep. The five-year-old, four-cylinder Mazda lacked the power to maintain speed. I feared for my children's lives as the car decelerated more and more as we ascended the hill. With the gas pedal pressed to the floor, the car slowed to twenty miles per hour.

My heart dropped to the floor as I tried to anticipate the appropriate maneuver for a car rolling backward in the slightly heavy traffic. I wondered if I could hit the brakes fast enough to prevent a collision. As I entertained these thoughts, I continued to converse with the children to conceal my fear. One second into a full-blown panic that the car would begin to roll down the hill, things changed. We made it to the top of the pass and began to pick up speed. I expressed no concern to the children, but my racing heart and sweaty armpits made me regret this independent trip without Sentwali. As soon as I arrived at my sister's house, I told her I could not drive that car back home over Raton Pass. I refused to put my children in danger and arranged for a rental car for our return trip. I let my nephew keep the Mazda since he had no car.

The visit to Albuquerque marked my first interaction with my sister's husband since my disclosure to her. We all pretended nothing ever happened, but the body remembers what the mind ignores. On my third day visiting my sister, I had a fainting spell. My sister had not assisted me with a fainting spell since my first one in church when I was fourteen years old. She knew I still had them but had not been with me when they occurred. Fortunately, we were at her house, and I just lay down for the customary two-hour recovery period. The next day we went about enjoying our vacation time.

In the back of my mind, I wondered why my sister did not leave her husband. I thought she was biding her time. She could not possibly love this man who sexually abused her little sister. I did not know what would make her believe she deserved no better than a man who betrayed her trust and hurt her family. Thus, I asked her if she had told her husband that she knew what he had done. She replied that she asked him about it years ago when I disclosed and he admitted it. I became silent from the pain of not being chosen. I numbed myself and shrank a little more.

CHAPTER 49

*C*e ran low on money fairly soon after moving to
Colorado. We were still paying for Sentwali's
master's degree and my car, in addition to rent and food. We
bought mostly used clothing for our growing children and did not
splurge on anything. Our savings dwindled fast, and we felt the
pressure on our marriage. I could not work additional hours
because I homeschooled the children. In the evening, I edited
Sentwali's school papers, which provoked arguments. I became
the embodiment of Dr. Carolyn Whitlow and would refer to his
writings as drafts, asking for at least two before I thought he
should turn in a paper. Learning to write hurts the ego and he did
not like doing things my way. By the end of his first year, two
significant changes occurred.

First, Sentwali secured an internship as a residence hall director, which meant we could move on campus and avoid paying
rent. We also would have a university meal plan for the family.
None of the students in his cohort had children, and I assumed his
advisors considered this hardship as well as his previous experience. We were grateful. They assigned him the largest residence

hall because it had a two-bedroom apartment to accommodate the children.

Second, Sentwali influenced me to apply to graduate school, insisting I should be writing my papers instead of editing his. He married me for my brain, and he liked to see me use it. He would feel uncomfortable being addressed as "doctor" if I did not share the title. I told Sentwali I would talk to the Psychology Department to see what programs they offered. As Sentwali studied in the higher education administration program, we would be of little help to one another. I took the required GRE and scored high enough for unconditional admission. I then met with the dean of the college to learn about the program offerings.

My two degrees prepared me primarily for clinical psychology; however, I vowed never to work with survivors again. I knew I could not study clinical psychology and risk a repeat of my master's program. I desired nothing to do with counseling because I needed to keep my pain safely buried. Of course, I did choose not to discuss that with the dean or with Sentwali. Instead, I applied to the educational psychology program that focused on teaching and learning principles and research. I believed I could use what I learned to help educate our children.

I developed a plan to complete the coursework in two years and the dissertation a year later in order to graduate with Sentwali, who liked the plan as well. The chair of the educational psychology program suggested I brush up on my statistics before beginning the program, as it required several courses in advanced statistics. More than ten years had passed since I earned the A in statistics at Cornell. Thus, I took his advice and enrolled in a course at the community college that summer. I received an A with little effort and became excited about being back in the classroom.

We moved into the residence hall in August before the semester began. Living on campus made it easy for Sentwali and me to schedule our courses, library time, and childcare responsibilities with a little help from a few undergraduate students who did not mind babysitting now and again. We rarely saw Bernie and the sisters anymore and, when we did, I picked the girls up to bring them to campus. We had enough student babysitters to no longer need Bernie's help.

We all adjusted well to living on campus. We lived on the ground floor and could enter directly into the apartment from outside, avoiding the lobby. The children rode their bikes more frequently because I no longer had to carry them downstairs. As a family we ate breakfast, lunch, and dinner daily, without my having to cook. Sentwali occasionally baked dessert in the apartment, but the small kitchen did not allow for extensive meal preparation, nor did our budget.

College campuses celebrate everything, so the children learned even more about the world. St. Patrick's Day, Halloween, Yom Kippur and our favorite, Kwanzaa, were all acknowledged in one way or another, not to mention my children's birthdays. Students made them Valentine cards, took them trick-or-treating throughout the hall, gave them Christmas gifts, and helped plan their parties.

During Christmas break the campus turned into a ghost town and we decided to drive back to Wisconsin to spend the holiday with Sentwali's family. Two days before Christmas my brother Mitchell called me at my mother-in-law's house. He asked me Pam's last name. He had known her as Pam Carter but knew she had gotten married. I told him "Selby." He spelled it out to make sure, and I impatiently confirmed. He then reported, "I'm sorry, she's not with us anymore." More impatient, I asked him what he meant, thinking she had moved out of Philadelphia and my mother wanted to send her a Christmas card, yet fearing the truth he meant. "She's gone. She's not with us anymore." My heart dropped as I understood clearly the meaning of his words.

A hundred thoughts ran through my mind simultaneously, not about Pam but about life, my life, my belief about good and evil, heaven and hell, God or no God. I inquired about the details of her death and he explained what he knew from the evening news. A Philadelphia police officer returned to his home last evening to discover his wife dead from two bullet wounds to the back of the head.

No one can prepare for a call announcing the sudden death of a loved one; it shocks the system. Pam had remained my best friend for twenty years, and we had spoken two months before Mitchell's call. Pam and I both shared burdens that made the conversation heavy. I had disclosed to her about my sexual abuse, even my sister's husband, and she had revealed knowledge of her husband's affair.

Pam had planned to divorce her husband after Christmas, but she wanted her daughter to spend one more holiday with both parents. She told me when she confronted her husband about the affair, he became upset. She walked away from him and went into her room because "he looked like he wanted to kill me." Her husband had never before said a wrong word to her or raised his voice before then. He typically displayed a calm and quiet demeanor with a sense of humor.

Pam's husband had been spending more time away from home and she wanted to find out why. She investigated and discovered the affair, provoking a side of him unfamiliar to her as he admonished her audacity to check into his whereabouts. Along with my shock, a rush of guilt flooded through me, as I realized I should have been more concerned when she said he looked as though he wanted to kill her. I would make sure to share this information with the family.

I spent Christmas with Sentwali's family in Wisconsin and flew to Philly a day later, still in shock. I spent as much time with Pam's family as possible, helping with all of the arrangements and talking through what we believe had happened. They also suspected her husband and we began to put the pieces together, specifically the fact that his ex-wife would not allow him to know her whereabouts. The bullet wounds were indicative of someone with expert shooting experience, such as an ex-marine like her husband.

The killer had murdered Pam in her sleep. Her family continued to be cordial to her husband but let their suspicions be known. They were careful not to do or say anything that would interfere with the ongoing investigation. The police considered him a suspect but did not have enough evidence to lock him up. Her husband walked free for more than a year before he finally went to trial and the jury found him guilty.

CHAPTER 50

*C*lasses resumed about three weeks after Pam's funeral. I tried my best to pull myself together, but could not stop wondering why God had taken her and not me. I could find no justification as to why someone as incredible as Pam would leave before me since I did not want to be alive. Through tears one day, I asked God, "Why did you take her and not me?" I did not expect an answer, but I felt a still voice in my heart that faintly whispered, "I have work for you to do." That voice did not resolve my anger or my sadness; it fueled disbelief instead.

I cried alone and often, always making sure Sentwali and the children were asleep or out of the apartment. One morning I went to my 8:00 class, arriving early to have time to settle down after taking care of the children's morning routine of breakfast and baths. This particular morning, I could not stop the tears. They simply came uncontrollably out of my eyes in discord from my intention.

My professor was the only person present because the rest of the students came only minutes before class began. I apologized for crying and told her my best friend had died recently. She offered me permission to cry without apologizing and said I did not have to remain in class. I insisted on being there because I felt unfit to be around my children or my husband. I had no family available and did not feel close enough to friends to share my grief. I pursued scholarship as the only worthwhile distraction.

I asked my brother David to visit me, and it took two months to make arrangements for him to receive dialysis in Colorado. He received four-hour treatments three times a week and had to coordinate with his doctors, insurance company and the dialysis center nearest me. We also had to wait for warmer weather for him to move about with ease. The school year went by quickly, and summer had come before we knew it. To stay on track, Sentwali and I took the same statistics course, the only class that overlapped our programs. We needed a consistent babysitter for the summer, and having David around would fulfill that need.

I drove David to dialysis and picked him up. He used his handyman skills to set up our television to access movie channels. We took him to church on Sundays. He enjoyed going to Walmart and riding around on the electronic wheelchairs. He used an electric chair when he was home in Philly but could not transport it to Colorado. He traveled with only his cane. We lived just over an hour from Rocky Mountain National Park and frequently visited what we called "God's playground." We were eager for David to see it, and Bernice's visit for a few days presented an excellent opportunity to take him to the park.

The scenic drive to the park is distinguished by curves, canyons, streams, trails, and boulders that wind up to over eleven thousand feet. At the peak is a visitor center with breathtaking views of the mountains. From there, visitors climb another one thousand feet on the rocky terrain of uneven steps that are difficult even for those in good health. The challenge of this stairway to heaven adventure would be worth every moment, so I thought.

I tried to describe to David what the peak looked like and offered him the option to try it, not taking into account the change of temperature as we ascended. David got about halfway up and began to struggle with the walk even with our assistance. But, he insisted on continuing. We eventually reached the peak, but his body disagreed with his decision. We could not stay at the top for even five minutes because the cold and damp weather for an acute lupus patient may as well have been kryptonite.

I had no time to address my fears and held back my tears trying to get David back down safely and watching his body become weaker and stiffer. I had flashbacks of Raton Pass when David 'decelerated' quickly. Bernice made sure the children were OK while I held onto David and got him to the car safely. His body could not reset itself, requiring us to call an ambulance for him later that night when he could not move and displayed extreme pain. I spent the next five days by his side in the hospital, full of regret and fearful my mother would never again trust me with his care.

David thanked me for the life-threatening journey and appreciated my willingness to challenge him. People often focused on his frailty, but he valued a challenge. Being on the mountain was probably something he would not be able to do again. He figured if he was unlikely to die of old age, he may as well live as much of his life as possible. He was accustomed to hospitals, mishaps, and setbacks and flare-ups, never blaming me for being overzealous in showing him the world.

CHAPTER 51

The following Christmas Bernice invited us to be with her family in Albuquerque and we accepted because she planned to move back to Philly after her husband retired the next year. Sentwali drove this time, and we rented a car for safety, arriving a few days before Christmas so Bernice and I could do some shopping. Ryan was an adult but still her only child, so she had several gifts for him. She also bought a considerable amount of presents for my children. The principle of reciprocity meant I had to buy gifts for all of her family members, including her husband; here I go again buying gifts for violators. Strangled by my silence, I had a fainting spell the day after Christmas.

My fainting spells had become so frequent and severe that Sentwali never trusted me in bathrooms, where they frequently began. The first year we moved to Colorado I saw a doctor about it. He diagnosed me with irritable bowel syndrome, as the spells usually began with constipation, then diarrhea, and stomach cramping that became increasingly severe over a thirty-minute period until I passed out. The stomach cramping signaled me to the bathroom with an attempt to relieve myself. In public places, Sentwali usually sent my daughter to the bathroom with me. If not, he would send her to check on me if I took too long. He automatically woke from his sleep whenever I got out of bed in the middle of the night to use the bathroom. My husband came to my rescue in my sister's bathroom while she took care of the children.

A few days after I returned home, Bernice called to check on me and mentioned that she noticed I fainted both times I came to her house. She asked if I thought her husband triggered the spells. Her question shocked me. Was it a trick question? Rhetorical? She had made it clear to me that she had no intention of choosing me over this man when she told me he admitted what he had done. She had chosen the man who betrayed her over the little sister who idolized her. There was nothing left to discuss; I had committed fully to living in the space of silence with her, for her, and to pretending I was strong enough to survive sexual assault in silence for the rest of my life.

Her choosing me would be my only solace other than her husband's death. The pain of not being chosen above corrupt individuals had hurt as much as the sexual abuse. Living in silence out of shame had hurt less than living in silence after my disclosure. No one responding to my pain with any attempt to rescue me felt as though I was drowning in an ocean of confusion and negligence. I could not see the shore, nor swim to safety. My sister asked me if I was drowning as she watched me sink. A drowning person cannot talk and swim at the same time. "No, it's not because of Robin." I shrunk a little more.

CHAPTER 52

*A*fter my dissertation committee accepted my research proposal, I met with them immediately to review my plans to graduate the following year. Two of the three committee members expressed concern with my timeline, as no student had ever completed the degree in three years. On average, it took nearly seven years to complete the program. I told them I needed to leave Colorado when my husband finished his program and they reminded me that he began his program a year before me. Sarcastically, I alleged, "Yes, but I'm smarter than him." They just looked at me, as if they did not know "most wives are smarter than their husbands." I wanted to say it tongue-in-cheek but thought I should quit already with the claim about my marriage.

I asked them to identify the part of my timeline they doubted because I could commit to staying on track as long as they would commit to the requested turn-around time to read my material. One committee member supported me without reservation, Dr. Cynthia Tyson. She had resigned from the university after teaching for only a year. I petitioned the Psychology Department to allow her to remain on my committee, and they approved despite her teaching at another university. Grateful she remained a voice of reason throughout the process, Dr. Tyson became a mentor and a friend.

I submitted the first draft of my research proposal to my chair, Dr. Teresa McDevitt. Having taken a few classes with her, I found her to be thoughtful, supportive, and reasonable. However, reading through all of her criticism of my writing led me to conclude otherwise, and I became furious with what I interpreted as nitpicking. I contacted Dr. Tyson to complain and she graciously allowed me to vent about the quality of my writing skills, as Dr. Whitlow had made certain of that. The Psychology Department wanted to sabotage my success, I protested. Dr. Tyson spoke softly and deliberately, similar to my professor who made me repeat the counseling course. The harsher the criticism, the softer they both spoke.

Dr. Tyson responded that she had seen many students similar to me. She clarified, "Students who think they already know it all, especially think they know how to write, never earn their degree." She told me she had completed her doctoral program with ease because she knew she lacked skills in some areas. Therefore, whatever her advisors, professors or others told her she should learn to do, she did so without question. In other words, Dr. Tyson offered me a choice between my Ivy League ego or the path of humility that would guarantee the completion of my timeline. I chose the path of humility, first apologizing to Dr. McDevitt as Dr. Tyson had advised. I also put my trust in Dr. McDevitt to guide me through the dissertation process, as Dr. Tyson had recommended.

The 1999 school year began with both Sentwali and I working on our dissertations. We divided our time between the dining hall, the campus recreation center, and the library, going to the dining hall as a family for all three meals. Sentwali and I took turns with the other activities, such as going to the gym, as we were trying to lose weight before graduation. I enjoyed step aerobics so much that I began teaching it for fun. In addition, I would run a mile around the track while processing the feedback from committee members.

Sentwali and I had difficulty negotiating sufficient library time. We both needed extensive time and dimes to retrieve and copy research articles, as well as time to write. I stayed up late at night working because my days were spent homeschooling the children while Sentwali worked. We knew we needed to take full advantage of Christmas break to complete our dissertations. We decided Sentwali would stay on campus by himself and I would go to Philly with the children. In Philly, I would have all the support needed to write while my mother helped with the children.

Our family and friends could not believe Sentwali and I had chosen to be apart for the holidays at a time when much of the world gathered close out of fear of Y2K. The anticipation of the year 2000 concerned Americans due to a reliance on technology. The internet, with limited information, was not as it is today. We used floppy disks that stored much smaller amounts of data compared to what is stored on a flash drive. Affluent individuals or businessmen only were able to afford laptops, and desktops were twice the size of today's version. All of the computer equipment was separate; microphones, cameras, and keyboards were not built in. Automation was relatively new. People manually locked their car doors and changed their clocks by hand to accommodate daylight savings. Most people wrote checks to pay bills, and the largest home television included a thirty-six-inch display through an enormous tube.

Rumors began to spread that the World Wide Web, now generally referred to as "the internet," was incapable of changing all four digits on the calendar. Computers identified years by the last two digits, with the assumption that the first two were "19." The year 1962 appeared as "62." Therefore, the world feared a grave technology malfunction that would set us back a hundred years. Many worried that we would have no water or food and stocked up on bottled water and canned goods to prepare for a disaster. Sentwali and I decided to work on our dissertation defenses while the rest of the world waited for the apocalypse. He stayed in Colorado, with his twenty cans of tuna and five gallons of water, while I went to Philly for a month.

My family supported me by helping to care for my children, bringing me Philly chicken cheese steaks from my favorite shop, letting me borrow their cars to go to the public library, and doing anything else I requested. The children behaved well and did not ask for much. We spent New Year's Eve at home and witnessed the dull moment on television as the New York City Time Square ball dropped. Two weeks later we were back in school for the final push toward graduation.

Sentwali's mother and oldest sister came for the ceremony to watch him deliver the student speech, an honor bestowed upon two students. David and Bernice returned to watch me receive an award for "dissertation of the year," another honor bestowed to two students. One month after graduation Sentwali and I packed the family in our minivan and drove back across the country to return to upstate New York as Drs. Ronald Sentwali and Rosenna Bakari. I accepted a tenure-track professor position at a state university, and Sentwali took an administrative position at the nearby private college.

Moving to upstate New York meant being closer to my family again and seeing them more often. I visited them and they visited me. My godson Danny spent several weeks with me in the summer and my children even met my father. My parents separated the year after Sentwali and I got married. Though we married on their anniversary we never got to share the occasion. My mother became less and less accepting of my father's hypocrisy, and my father began to threaten her. My sister Gwen physically interfered at one point to keep my father from hurting my mother. When my mother began to fear him, she called the police and had him removed from the house. However, she continued to care for him, as his body became increasingly feeble. She took the children and me to see him on one of our visits, enjoying a pleasant stay with a weak man who finally lost his power to harm. He passed away about a year after our visit. My mother arranged and paid for his funeral. She showed him this last act of kindness out of strength, not weakness. I admired her for that.

Mom lived a life of compassion. She showed me the difference between seeking power over others and being self-empowered. She never tried to control my father, she simply tired of him controlling her.

PART IV

Compounded pain is the reality of denial. Survivors tend to avoid pain by denying it or by ignoring it. We become accustomed to building a life around the pain and forget it is there. After all, that's the point of denial and avoidance; focusing on other things or finding ways to numb out. Unfortunately, we set ourselves up for the "compounded pain effect." When regular life pain comes our way, as it does, it attaches to the denied pain. All other experiences are filtered through that trauma. Even ordinary pain brings extraordinary grief. Sometimes, in the space of compounded pain, we stumble across the healing path, alas.

CHAPTER 53

*a*fter three years of living in upstate New York, we moved to Iowa for my husband to take an administrative position at a private university while I focused on homeschooling our children. I chose the unschooling approach to homeschooling over the traditional method. Traditional homeschooling focuses on a formally prepared curriculum to educate students at home. Unschooling does not use a formal curriculum. Everything we did as a family fostered learning, not only academic knowledge but building character, integrity, commitment, kindness, responsibility, and citizenship. Grocery shopping, banking, cooking, and attending community events were as educational as our reading, writing, and math lessons. I also required physical education, allowing both children to choose their sport after they learned to swim. My daughter developed a passion for swimming and continued private lessons. My son decided on martial arts, tae kwon do (TKD). Fortunately, the nearby YMCA offered both of those activities and we spent most of our evening there. Nailah went to swim practice daily; the TKD program provided instruction three times a week.

After two weeks of sitting in the back of the gym waiting for the TKD class to end, I decided to join. I liked that the instructor required the students to learn the academics of the art. He quizzed them on the required Korean history and the history of TKD, as well as the TKD pledge and the tenets, courtesy, integrity, perseverance, self-determination, and indomitable spirit. Students' incorrect responses resulted in push-ups or sit-ups for adults and children alike.

I did not wait to order a uniform to join the class. I just lined up in the back of the class one day and followed along. The large class size put me five rows back, out of sight from the rest of the students, so I did not feel embarrassed by my mistakes or by my lack of appropriate attire. I had not exercised since leaving Colorado, and the thought of exercising never occurred to me while living in New York. Martial arts seemed to be an effective means to get back into shape and to eliminate the boredom of waiting for my son.

After struggling during the first week with the physical requirements of the class, I stepped on a scale and realized I weighed the same as when I carried my second child ten years ago. The weight crept up on me while we were living in New York. In addition to not working out, the doctor had put me on Zoloft for clinical depression the last year we lived there.

My medical doctor diagnosed me after I complained about mental confusion, irritation, and hyper sensitivity, which manifested into a lack of patience with my children. I noticed myself yelling at them often, which felt unusual. I expressed my frustration more with tone than volume but knew my reaction did not reflect my children's behavior. They were smart and exceptionally well-behaved. I also found myself crying at work for no reason. My doctor contributed my symptoms to perimenopause. However, I did not tell her, nor think of it myself at the time, that the more likely trigger dealt with the increased contact with family members. I visited Philly more often and saw James each time, and sometimes Robin. I had gone back to spending holidays with my violators.

The Zoloft eased my symptoms after about a week, but, reluctant to rely on medication, I quit taking it after a couple of months. The doctor never recommended anything other than the drug to deal with the depression. Unfortunately, within a week of missing the Zoloft, all of my symptoms returned, and I resumed taking it as prescribed until we moved to Iowa. By then I had put on an extra twenty pounds. Once we left New York, I never opened the bottle.

We loaded up the van with our personal belongings, including: our dog, one cat and her litter of four kittens, two children, my husband and me. We drove the seventeen hours straight to our new home because no hotel could accommodate us with the pets. I hoped the change of environment would settle my brain and alleviate my symptoms, as TKD offered a welcomed change. The depression subsided, and I valued my new life far away from the men who violated me.

The instructor ended one of my first classes with a command of thirty sit-ups and twenty push-ups, adding that we could dismiss ourselves after completing the tasks. I thought I would be there all night. I felt punished, not motivated. I did not personally know any woman my age who could do thirty sit-ups and twenty push-ups. I wondered whether he wanted us to quit, for most of us seemed to struggle. I did the push-ups as best I could and returned determined to bond with my son, learn to defend myself, and get in shape. Overcoming challenges came almost second nature to me.

My son loved the program. He instinctively remembered the forms and picked up on the Korean commands the instructor called out to direct our actions. I enjoyed all of the TKD movements, but I hated the traditional fitness that involved the jumping jacks, push-ups, sit-ups, and running around the gym. I joined other fitness classes during the week to get in shape for TKD. In fact, I worked out every day, doing step aerobics, weight training, or walking on the treadmill on the days I did not have TKD. I could remain invisible for only so long as the only Black adult female in the program.

Hitting and kicking people felt good. My brothers taught me how to fight as a child when we lived in the projects, and I had my share of adolescent brawls. Luckily, I never harmed anyone too badly or got injured. I had enough fights that sparring in class felt natural to me, although we did not spar regularly, maybe only ten minutes a week. I found it cathartic to throw kicks and punches in the air while screaming as well. However, the instructor's use of hypothetical situations of sexual assault when demonstrating the use of techniques made me uncomfortable. He spoke with the assumption that no one in the class had experienced those circumstances or unaware that his language might trigger a survivor. I imagined my sister's husband with every new scenario. My desire to heal emerged with my confidence to defend myself.

CHAPTER 54

One day while at the library with the children, I browsed the section on spirituality and wellness. A CD box for the book, *The Power of Now* by Eckhart Tolle, caught my attention in the New Author section. Although we occasionally took the children to church, I became less inspired by sermons based in fear with a focus on male dominance. I had as many negative church experiences as positive ones. When we first moved to Iowa, I attended a church and joined their women's Sunday School class. One day, I referenced God with the use of a feminine pronoun. The teacher and other women were confused by my statement although the context specified God as the subject. My unconventional feminine reference to God stirred a conversation that no one in the class addressed beyond pointing out the blasphemy in my language. I frustrated them, and they disappointed me with their insistence that God must be referenced as male and identified as an external deity. I dropped the conversation and began a slow withdrawal from religious affiliation after irregularly attending two more churches over the next two years.

I wanted to feel empowered inside. Throughout my life, I watched men draw on their internal sense of power and women give theirs away. I could not separate the imbalance of power between genders from my experience of sexual abuse. Each time I walked into a church, the imbalance of power stifled me. Masculine references like "Our Father," "Praise Him," and "Bless the Lord" filled men with pride and entitlement every Sunday, as clergy told them to lead the country, their families, and to reign over women. I could not feel the freedom of God, and began to rebel against the request for my obedience to male dominance.

My mother had told me to pray for truth and I concluded I would not find it in a church. I had read the Bible from cover to cover while living in New York, but discovered no resolutions, only questions that clergy could not answer beyond denominational interpretations. Religious protocol and concepts had little to do with God and everything to do with cultural standards, all designed by men. I yearned to broaden my search for the truth about God, the connection to humanity, and to my pain.

I listened to *The Power of Now* every night as I fell asleep and began to read books by Deepak Chopra on spirituality. I came to understand God as energy, neither male nor female, except when reflected within us. I began to see God as a reflection of myself and to see myself as a reflection of God. I slowly stopped trying to find God and started to be God. Only by being God could I identify the God in others. I accepted that God exists only through connections. The more connections I make, the more I reflect God. In a world where I had always felt disconnected, I began the slow journey of trying to connect. I continued my search for truth through a spiritual rather than a religious practice.

I meditated, read, and talked with friends who sought God without fear. I searched for authors who spoke about God outside a religious context. Deepak Chopra, Eckhart Tolle, Caroline Myss, and Oriah Mountain Dreamer invited me into myself, which is the best view from which to see others. Connecting with others meant I had to learn to connect first with myself.

I noticed that whenever I disclosed my disinterest in religion, people immediately tried to defend God, never asking about my belief in God. People assumed that if I disconnected from the church, I disconnected from God. I feel the opposite to be true. I feel sorry for people who go to church to find God as I did. I also feel sorry for those who believe they need to defend God, as God would have to be pretty small to need defending. The God I found within me cannot be diminished by anything human beings say or believe. While I have tried to express my beliefs about God I never tried to defend God, no more than I would advocate for gravity. No one would protect gravity, and most people know little about how it works. We understand only that it is critical to our existence on earth. The same with God: God, in my understanding, is the totality of the universe and exists limitlessly beyond any belief we hold.

CHAPTER 55

o my surprise, everything I learned in TKD supported
my growing understanding of living a spiritual life. An
important principle of self-defense is to go with the flow. Martial
artists learn to go with the natural flow of energy. For instance, if
someone is pulling your hair, the instinct to pull away would
result in severe pain. Such a response leaves the attacker with a
handful of your hair. Rather than pulling away, the defense most
consistent with natural energy flow is to firmly press the attacker's hand to your head to prevent pain. As you hold their hand to
your head, pain-free, you then execute your offensive move with
your free hand. We learned to pay attention to the way limbs bend
and to follow that direction to avoid broken arms and legs, as well
as to oppose the direction to break a limb. We practiced falling to
the ground safely by using the natural flow of energy. Resist the
urge to resist and go with the flow. Contrary to what the
untrained mind tells you, the safest self-defense is synchronicity
with the flow of energy rather than resistance. Learn to respond,
not react. A reaction comes from the mind's fear as a response to a
threat. Responses come from letting go of the mind's apprehen-
sion and responding from a sense of knowing. After numerous

failures to execute a technique, the instructor would utter "Too much mind," to remind me to focus, not fear.

Eckhart Tolle also identified the mind as the culprit of much of our problems. What the undisciplined mind tells us to do when we feel emotionally threatened is contrary to what moves us forward. I began to practice allowance in my spiritual life, along with the flow of energy in my martial arts. As I advanced in TKD ranking, I developed an understanding of "the power of now." The present moment always holds higher potential than any prior experience. The most significant potential manifests in the absence of resistance when I go with the flow.

I tried a guided meditation to increase my internal sense of power. However, the repetitive motion of kicking took a toll on my knee joints, which made finding a comfortable position for meditation painful, almost as painful as keeping my mind still for ten minutes. The effort to empty my mind turned up the volume on my mind chatter. I would think about what the children needed from me, how soon David could visit, our depleted finances from me not working, and why my sister never left her husband. I understood that rambling thoughts did not diminish the value of meditation. However, I found martial arts to be more supportive of my emotional competence.

In TKD I could focus my energy on one thing and feel calmer than when I tried to focus my mind on nothing. I focused on the ideal target to land my punch or my kick, the accuracy of my technique to break a board, or my breath to build my stamina. I saw a one-hundred-pound woman break a one-inch wooden board with ease. I yearned for that type of focus and worked for it. I practiced daily on my physical movements and my mental focus. TKD became part of my spiritual practice for this reason. Soon, the sit-ups and push-ups were no longer a challenge. I wish I could say the same for my developing spiritual practice; it took much more time.

TKD sessions lasted for ten weeks, with an option to test for advancement at the end. I felt confident about testing for my yellow belt after adapting to the demanding physical expectations. I knew my required form and my academics. I had also lost fifteen pounds. We tested on a Saturday, and the instructor announced the results in class on Tuesday. He called students who promoted by name. One by one, they walked to the front of the class to greet the instructor and receive their new belt.

The instructor called my name last and said he had a special announcement. As I stood in front of the class, he praised me for my commitment to training and my skill level, and then advanced me from white to orange belt, skipping the yellow belt. He augmented the gesture by divulging that only twice in over ten years had he granted a student a double promotion. I thanked him and accepted my new belt, which I had not yet learned to tie properly. I asked the instructor if I could speak to him after class.

After class, I expressed my disappointment to him about the double promotion, as I wanted to be a regular student like everyone else. I struggled to meet his expectations, always feeling inadequate. He then informed me my performance exceeded his expectations and rewarded me with more work, which made no sense at the time.

I resented him singling me out when I tried to remain unseen. The instructor expressed surprise at my reaction to the recognition and emphasized he had granted only two students a double promotion in twenty years of teaching. He hoped I would accept within myself what he saw in me. I accepted that the double promotion meant I had the responsibility of learning the requirements for two belt levels by the next testing date, only ten weeks.

The white belt form had nineteen movements, and I found the pattern tough to memorize. The yellow and orange belt forms had twenty-one and twenty-four movements, respectively. Learning both forms in ten weeks required twice the practice time, but I did it. I became fully committed to being the best martial artist possible to prove to myself that what the instructor saw in me was real talent; focus and flow became my mantra.

CHAPTER 56

$\mathcal{T}$he move to Iowa put us far away from my family, but within driving distance of Sentwali's family. Thus, we spent holidays at his mother's house in Wisconsin. We spent our first summer vacation at a resort not far from her home after visiting her for a couple of days. Three days into our one-week summer vacation my family called to inform me David had been hospitalized and had slipped into a coma.

We had been trying to make plans for him to visit Iowa, but he had not been well enough and too sick to receive a kidney transplant. Although I had volunteered to give him a kidney, the doctor said David's body would still reject a transplant organ due to the numerous blood transfusions he had received over the years. He would have to remain on dialysis for the rest of his life. His graft that allowed for the administration of dialysis again became infected and caused all of his organs to malfunction. This time the doctor offered no prognosis for David, but I told my mother I would make arrangements to come to Philly after we returned from our vacation.

Several hours after receiving the news about David, I began to have vivid visions of him that I could not get out my mind. He appeared jovial and playful talking directly to me, telling me not to worry about him. I could feel his presence for hours as if he were right next to me. I continued to behave as normal in interactions with my husband and children while having this strange experience with David.

As my day came to an end and I finally got some alone time, I heard David express thoughts of leaving, the way Pam and my father had left. This telepathic communication with David in his coma felt like the most natural interaction ever. I told him our mother would never let him go, and he replied by giving me the responsibility of convincing her to let him go. I offered my internal response: "I can't do that."

I felt my soul darken, as I believed I could never tell my mother to take her son off life support. I could not rationalize my mystical experience with David and I tried to dismiss it. The rest of the week did not feel like a vacation. I felt burdened. I tried to explain the metaphysical events to my husband, but he insisted that David would recover as usual. He had been in and out of hospitals enough to have become used to it. I wanted Sentwali to be right, but I could not deny my connection with David.

David had been in a coma for five days when I arrived at his side, and the doctor had given my mother the prognosis. David's brain had no significant neural activity. Earlier in the day they had resuscitated him to keep his heart pumping. I took one look at him and knew he had let go of this world. When he first became ill, he told me he would fight to live as long as he could move around on his own. He never wanted to be bound to a wheelchair. The last time the doctors replaced his graft, they had warned him that he had no more possible placements site in his upper body. The next time the graft failed, the new one would have to be placed in his healthy leg, and consequently, would confine David to a wheelchair. When I realized the situation with the graft, I understood why he chose to leave. He had no written will and my mother, his next of kin, could not carry the burden of deciding on his death. I knew I had to honor David's visit with me.

The medical staff insisted resuscitation is unnecessary physical trauma to a body. One nurse admonished the family for not having an end-of-life plan for someone as ill as David had been for the past ten years. I matched her level of insensitivity as I reminded her our family needed to make decisions without her interference. Still, I found comfort in her stance because she confirmed what I knew David had chosen.

Bernice and I stayed at the hospital. We sat in the lobby and discussed the doctor's recommendation to remove life support and allow David to go peacefully. I told Bernice of my metaphysical visit from him and his request. She agreed to support me in requesting my mother remove him from life support. Contemplating losing David felt surreal, even though I made it so practical, objective, and emotionless. I wanted him to have his last wish and refused to feel the pain of my decision. I had become skilled at denying myself pain.

I convinced my mother to take him off life support, as the doctors had recommended. She cried at my request but agreed to take a vote from all the siblings before she signed the papers. Mom also wanted to make sure all of us had a chance to visit with David before he passed. No one objected, as we all thought he had suffered enough.

Mom asked her pastor to visit David one last time and consult with the family. The pastor prayed for David's soul and guidance for the family. After my mother signed the papers, she left the hospital because she could not stand to witness David taking his last breath. I sat by his side with my sister Bernice while the nurse came in to take him off life support. She also gave him an injection of morphine to help him permanently sleep. I watched someone die for the first time. I watched with silent envy, wishing I had departed before him.

CHAPTER 57

$\mathcal{I}$ remained strong for my mother as we planned her youngest son's funeral. I could still feel his presence and knew I had fulfilled his request. None of us cried too much because we knew how difficult life had become for David over the years. He never felt sorry for himself and would not want us to feel sorry for him. So, I didn't. Instead, I helped settle the insurance, sent out announcements, picked out a casket and clothing and wrote his obituary. At least two other family members declared David had had a similar metaphysical visit with them before he passed. They described him the same as I saw him, jovial.

I held up well throughout the funeral. To my surprise, I even kissed David's forehead one last time during the family's final viewing of the body, which differed from my usual experience at funerals. At Pam's funeral, I did not view her body at all, as my heart could not take seeing her dead body. Viewing my father's body gave me a bit of relief. I believed his death would allow my mother to continue her life in peace. Still, I honored him with a poem about the positive lessons he taught me. All of the siblings agreed to speak at Dad's funeral, but only I got up to talk when the time came. I think we all just wanted to be done with that chapter of our lives. I do not believe I saw anyone cry other than my mother at Dad's funeral.

After viewing David's body, I returned to my seat with the rest of my siblings as the minister prepared to close the casket. As the coffin closed, I felt the onset of a panic attack. I felt my spirit jump out of my body and go into the casket with David, and a scream burst from within me. Like Jesus, I wept.

My body weakened and I could no longer stand up or even catch my breath. My brothers dragged my limp body out of the church and into the limousine as I sobbed. Darkness consumed me from within and I held my head down all the way to the grave-yard as I sat in my brother George's arms inside the limousine. At the grave site, I refused to get out of the car. I could do no more to participate in this cruel twist of fate.

Why did everyone get to go before me when I did not want to be here? How could I live the rest of my life without David? He had been my little big brother, my chess opponent, pick-up basketball coach, prom date, boyfriend monitor, housewarming guest, and my handyman. I had rescued him from the mountain, helped him to the bathroom, and pushed his wheelchair. I could not see a future without him. We had spent forty-two years together. First Pam died, now David. I did not want to go back to live in a city that he had never seen.

My brother George forced me out of the funeral car just as he had dragged me into it, insisting I participate fully. I resisted, but he physically pulled me in spite of my verbal, but unintelligible objection. At Pam's funeral, I never went near the casket. Now, I suffered compounded pain; I grieved for Pam and David. George put a flower in my hand to throw into the grave and every forced gesture drove me further and further into darkness.

Curbing my emotions of anger and pain took all my energy. The burden of saying goodbye to David made my unhealed heart too heavy. The intense feeling of abandonment made gestures of kind words, hugs, and handshakes seem hollow. I could not stay in my body to watch these happenings, returning to my mother's house in a zombie state, present in the body and absent in mind. The presence of one hundred people could not make up for the absence of the one I lost. Every sentiment spoken went in one ear and out the other, more likely, never even entering one ear. No matter how much food and drink served, I remained empty.

CHAPTER 58

I returned from Philly with a gaping hole in my heart that I believed nothing could fill. I focused on TKD and my fitness to try to fill the void in spite of the physical pain it manifested. I felt pain in my left hip that would not go away and went to my doctor, who sent me to an orthopedic specialist. After reviewing my x-rays, the specialist informed me I had osteoarthritis. Half of the cartilage in my hip had deteriorated. He explained no cure existed and I would ultimately require hip replacement surgery. He advised me to try to avoid surgery until I turned fifty because hip replacements last only twenty years. An artificial hip before age fifty would guarantee the need for another one if I lived past seventy. He further advised me to remain physically active and return when the pain became severe.

I added use of the treadmill to my fitness routine to warm up and lubricate my hip before TKD. I hated the treadmill but found it useful for this purpose. Twenty minutes on it felt like twenty hours. A friend encouraged me to run on it instead of walk. I eventually built up my stamina to three miles once a week, and the pain in my hip faded completely.

My depression remained, and I wondered how long I would

last without getting back on Zoloft. As long as I could avoid shouting at the children, I figured I would try to stay off the Zoloft. I distanced myself from the children to save them from the effects of my irritation, anxiety, and depression. I struggled daily to get out of bed. The children always woke before me and sometimes waited for hours for me to join them for homeschool. They patiently ate cereal, read and worked on writing assignments until I got out of bed.

I believed returning to Philly for Christmas would ease my depression. I also wanted to support my mother, as I suspected the holiday without my brother would be stressful. Sentwali agreed. After his school semester ended the four of us flew home. David had been dead for five months and being in the house without him made me sad. I could not breathe well, especially walking up the stairs. I felt a tightness in my chest as well. I just could not get a grip on myself. My body would not allow me to move beyond the trauma in my life.

The breathing difficulty remained after I returned home, and I went back to my doctor. She diagnosed asthma and prescribed a daily inhaler that consisted of a steroid, which worked wonders. My body performed so much better in TKD, and I could run the three miles on the treadmill much more comfortably.

Unfortunately, after about three months I noticed my knee joints feeling stiffer and could barely get out of bed in the mornings. I asked my doctor if stiff joints could be a side effect of the asthma medication. In spite of her assurance that the drug could not have that side effect, I looked online and found a site that had hundreds of similar complaints about the medication. It was not a medical site, but a discussion group. The prescription treated COPD and asthma; I had symptoms of only asthma. I requested to be taken me off of the medication, and the doctor respected my concern. She prescribed an inhaler for asthma, one less invasive to the body.

I do not understand why doctors are not more considerate of

how they prescribe drugs. My degree in psychology trained me to use the least invasive and restrictive technique as possible to get students to respond to learning. Students should take responsibility for their learning, with educators as the facilitator; I expected this approach from doctors as well. Offering the most potent prescription to remove a symptom may be equivalent to spanking a child to get them to behave. I sought to control my body with the least pharmaceutical intervention. I wanted to feel in synch with my body by connecting it to my mind, not to a pill or an inhaler or medical device.

I met a Black woman in the grocery store, a rare sight in Iowa, so we stopped to chat. We both had our pre-adolescent children with us. We lived on opposite sides of town, but she had stopped to shop while taking care of errands in my part of town. After getting to know one another for fifteen minutes, with our children becoming impatient, she invited me to join her running group of women. "We run at 5:00 every Wednesday. You should join us."

I had never run outside, only on the treadmill. I ran three miles, but her group ran six. She responded to my concern by contending six miles outdoors would feel easier than three miles on the treadmill, especially with a group. Desperate for community and distraction, I agreed to meet her the following Wednesday. In her farewell, she confirmed "I'll look for you Wednesday morning," a shocking reality, as I thought she meant 5:00 in the afternoon. I had enjoyed talking with her too much to reveal my misunderstanding, therefore, accepted the confirmation for a 5:00 a.m. run.

Enthusiastically prepared to meet a group of Black female athletes, I set my alarm clock for 4:30 a.m. to drive twenty minutes downtown for my first outdoor run. I did not brush my teeth or even wash my face; I just slipped into my running gear, grabbed my mp3 player and earphones and slipped out the door without waking anyone.

I arrived first, at 4:55 a.m., and my new friend Charlene came immediately afterward. When two more runners arrived, Charlene introduced me to the white women. I had heard the saying often, "When you assume, you make an ass out of u and me." I made an ass out of me that day. It turned out that neither Charlene nor I had any Black friends to share with one another. We both spent ninety percent of our social time in environments where we were the only Black female, which caused us to gravitate toward one another in the store.

In spite of my brief disappointment, I trusted Charlene's advice about the transition from indoor to outdoor running. The four of us trotted off slowly as the sun barely peaked at us. About a mile into the run I felt a shift from deep within as if my spirit had re-entered my body after months of absence. I ran around my comrades and asked how far ahead I could go because I wanted to pick up the pace a bit.

As the sun came up in its fullness, the sky opened up to the rhythm of my feet. I found joy in the cadence of my footsteps and the rhythm of Whitney Houston. "I'm Every Woman" played in my ear while conversations with David ran through my mind and almost made me forget about my comrades. I felt a shift in my sensory perception as all anxiety left my body and I felt in sync with the entire universe. The treadmill never made me feel anything other than pain and fatigue.

I slowed down so the women could see me. For safety reasons, we had agreed to remain in sight of each other. We ended our run with short affirmations of "see you next week." I drove home full of hope, crawled back in the bed and went to sleep. We met again and again and again; I became alive with each run.

One morning about a month after we began running together, the women angered me by not notifying me in advance of their plan to run eight miles. I loved running, but it felt like a challenge. I did not feel mentally or physically prepared to increase the distance. They told me to let them know if I became too tired. I started a few feet ahead of them, as usual, and kept my frustration to myself. About forty minutes into the run I heard them yelling to get my attention. I stopped to let them catch up, and they explained that I had run too far past the mid-mile-marker. As we were already four and a half miles out, we had to complete nine miles instead of eight because of my enthusiasm that day.

To my surprise, I loved the long run. Charlene also enjoyed it, so we added it to our weekly schedule. We ran nine by ourselves on Mondays and six with the other women on Wednesdays. The runner's high captured me. I had never tolerated drugs well, but my tolerance for the pangs of running increased with my runner's high. My knees hurt and I did not care. Shoes were expensive, yet I broke the budget on them anyway. The diagnosis of exercise-induced asthma did not deter me. I even ran as a treatment to lubricate my hip joints after the doctor had diagnosed me with arthritis. I set a goal to run one thousand miles the next year.

CHAPTER 59

O n the anniversary of David's death, I wrote to him in my journal, saying my sadness had begun to subside as I became used to not having him around after a year. I had stopped crying daily, at least. I might have felt more depressed except Iowa in July is beautiful. Sentwali worked forty hours a week instead of fifty, which he did during the semesters, and having him around the house more made me happier. More important, the year cycle meant I had managed my grief through all the days that triggered sadness of David's absence, his birthday, the holidays and the family reunion. Now I could begin to heal.

On a beautiful Saturday morning, just three days after I wrote to David about my grieving process, I received a phone call from Philly. Caller ID indicated my sister Bernice's phone number. I assumed she wanted to talk about the anniversary of David's death. I was upstairs watching television in bed, half-asleep, Sentwali was in the basement watching TV, and the children were not at home. Answering the phone to greet my sister, she abruptly redirected the conversation to tell me she had terrible news. Danny, our nephew and my godson, had died in a motorcycle accident. His motorcycle collided with a Philadelphia SEPTA transit bus.

I dropped the phone as I screamed and ran down two flights of stairs to my husband, sobbing. This news could not be real, I wished. Danny could not die at nineteen years old and I could not mourn another significant loss. I had lost my best friend, my father, my brother, and now my godson. I felt myself getting weaker with each death. I refused to quit. Every time I looked at my children I knew I had to fight and follow through on whatever plan God had for me.

I repeated with my sister Gwen what I had done with my mother to bury David twelve months prior. I also acted as the negotiator between my sister and her husband Joseph when conflict arose between them because he was not Danny's biological father. Her husband wanted more input into funeral arrangements, but there were enough cooks in the kitchen between the two birth families. I helped to keep my sister separated from her husband until after the funeral. She had enough family support for him to take a back seat.

Gwen and Joseph frequently argued, and their current disagreement surprised no one. He looked as though the stress of their marriage had taken a toll on him, as he had lost considerable weight since I last saw him at David's funeral. I asked him what he had done to lose so much weight and he replied that he had slightly modified his diet but the pounds seemed to drop naturally. He had even gone to the doctor to be sure he did not have any illness. The doctor found no medical concern.

The day after the funeral I went to Bernice's house to get away from everything. She and I had spent little time together in Philly, so going to her home for a visit sounded like a good idea. When I walked in, she told me her husband was in the bedroom resting, so, we spoke softly. He eventually came out to get some food and took it back to their room. Within thirty minutes of seeing him, the inevitable happened. My stomach began to cramp and I went to the bathroom. On the toilet, the pains got sharper and deeper as I sat there folded over with my head between my knees. The vomiting began, and I called out for Bernice to assist me. I believe we both realized the silence and the spells were a package deal. My body cried out with fainting spells, what my mouth could not speak.

$\mathcal{I}$ stayed with my family in Philly for over a week to grieve the loss of a young life, regretting sharing physical and emotional space with two men who violated me. Even when they were not in my presence, I listened to people speak fondly of them and act respectfully on their behalf; they unquestionably expected me to do the same. I returned to Iowa again in a deep depression. I did everything on automatic: workouts, reading with children, library time, math, and household chores. I could see the strain of my mental status on my daughter's face but could not muster the strength to be a better parent because I felt horrible inside. My daughter often would fix me food to eat and keep track of how many days I had not eaten. She would lay on the bed with me while I cried. My son began to fall into his own world from my neglect of his grief. Danny had been like a big brother who lived far away. He had taught my son how to play the newer video games, and David had been his favorite uncle. But I could not see anyone's pain but my own.

I cared for the children as best I could and hoped they understood my grief. I spent increasingly more time in my bedroom with minimum attention paid to their education. We read a lot and worked on math, but not much else. I made sure to pull myself together by the time my husband returned home from work so he would not notice my mental distress. I looked forward to 3:30 p.m. each day when I took my daughter to swim practice. Many of the parents watched their children practice. Not me; I worked out while Nailah practiced. Even during swim meets I would come into the pool area to watch during her race only. Sometimes I erred in my timing and missed her event. Other parents would tell me how great she raced, and I would express pride to my daughter as if I had seen her.

My grief became worse as regretful news kept coming. Three months after we buried Danny, the doctor diagnosed my sister Gwen's husband with pancreatic cancer. They had previously misdiagnosed him concerning his weight loss. My family prayed for a miracle that he would live beyond the doctor's prediction of fifteen months.

I struggled with anxiety and depression while trying to find ways to support my sister and grieve for myself. At least she lived near the rest of our family and could grieve with other family members. I had a husband who worked to distract himself from pain and conflict and children who needed more from me than I had to give. I knew few people in Iowa, no one well enough to share my pain. My family prepared to suffer the third death in three years.

Not knowing how to grieve, I threw myself into fitness even more. I began running twenty miles a week, added TKD classes by traveling to the alternate school site, and lifted weights regularly. I stopped eating by 4:00 p.m. on the evenings before my 5:00 a.m. runs twice a week to avoid the urge to use the bathroom. My weight dropped significantly and I started borrowing my thirteen-year-old daughter's clothing as mine were too large.

I worked out with the TKD instructor to prepare for my black belt test, still a year away. We became friends because we were both looking for a distraction from unstated, unshared pain. He had recently divorced. One day he noticed the solemn look on my face and asked if I was OK. I told him I did not want to talk about anything, but later in the day I called him on the phone and asked him to listen.

I had bought plane tickets to visit my family in Philly for Christmas while my husband planned to visit his family in Milwaukee. However, with David and Danny no longer present, I could not bear the thought of spending time with people who never honored the pain of my sexual abuse. Moreover, I did not want Bernice's husband to see me because the weight loss made me look similar to my appearance when he sexually abused me. I disclosed to my TKD instructor about the abuse and my family's response to it, including my attempt at freedom ten years ago when I wrote the letters to my sister and mother. I told him I had been silent since then and had no strength to bring it up again, but I was tired of being around my violators. I thought too much time had passed for me to raise concerns.

My instructor expressed disgust with my family and supported me beyond what anyone had ever offered to that point. He said he admired my strength and insisted I not go home and subject myself to people who ignored my pain. He reminded me that they knew what had happened but chose to protect the viola-tors. They did not deserve my company, nor another explanation from me. "No one should have to repeat what you just told me. So even if you told them ten years ago, you don't owe them another explanation," he angrily remarked. I had never thought about my abuse that way. He firmly stated that my family had plenty of time to show support and compassion. They had ignored my needs, which gave me the right to take care of myself. We had a long conversation and he helped me devise a plan B, and we never talked about the abuse again.

The children and I flew into Philly as planned, but I rented a car at the airport and drove to Baltimore to visit a friend instead of going to my mother's house. I made no apology to my family for our absence, and they did not ask.

CHAPTER 61

I met a woman at the gym named Rita who practiced energy work to heal physical and psychological trauma. I became curious, as I had spent time a year earlier with a healing practitioner, the uncle of one of my daughter's teammates. I talked to her mother about my knee pain from all the workouts, and she told me her brother might be able to offer some relief. She set up time for me to spend with him. She explained that he conducted sessions similar to a massage with clothing on, and transmitted energy into and out of the body as he worked. I had nothing to lose, so I said yes.

I made an appointment to go to the teammate's house to visit with the uncle after our introduction at a swim meet. I lay on his table, and he began to put his hands on my body. He started at my ankle with what felt like a gentle massage. As his hands approached my hips, he said softly, "I'm sorry for the bad things men have done to you." My eyes welled with tears. Those were the only words spoken during the entire session. I continued to have knee pain, but my heart opened a tiny bit.

I walked into Rita's office and began to complain about my husband and the people around me when she asked about my reason for consulting her. I told her my entire body felt stressed. After listening to me speak for about ten minutes, she ignored everything I stated and said, "I sense you have trouble with an older man. He could be your father or your brother." My eyes welled with tears. She knew nothing of the healer I had seen a year before, and he knew nothing of my professor from long ago who had sensed I was "hiding something." I could barely get anyone in my life to recognize my pain, yet two minutes in the company of someone with trained intuition made me transparent. I felt spellbound by Rita and could respond only with the truth.

I shared with her what I had shared with my TKD instructor. The emotionally intense session lasted about ninety minutes as I began to face my truth. Rita did not talk any longer than necessary before inviting me to connect with my inner child. She guided me in exploring the abuse as my seven-year-old self. I cried about the abuse for the first time I could remember.

I walked out of Rita's office with an understanding of what it meant for a seven-year-old to survive rape. I saw and felt the pain even though I could not remember the event. My mind and body ached profoundly as every muscle tensed up. The practice of allowance meant I could watch the pain and let it wash over me like a mighty ocean wave, which might knock me down and scrape my body against the sand, but I would end up back on the shore. I needed to trust this process, but the pain felt unbearable. I wanted desperately to die rather than landing on the shore broken again and again.

The suicidal ideation heightened for weeks after my session with Rita. I believe if I had not had children to care for, I would have killed myself but I had to stay to protect my children. I never wanted them to feel the abandonment I felt by a mother who still lived. Thus, I could not die, even though I did not know how to live.

I did not go back to see Rita for a while because I knew healing required deeper excavation of the pain. I could not tend to my children and my inner child, which needed far more attention than my children. I had little to give either of them. I sought counsel with Rita only when the weight of the burden in my life became as heavy as the burdens I faced in her office. I deliberately held onto denial.

CHAPTER 62

*A*s a source of distraction, in TKD I kicked faster, punched harder, and soaked up the academics like a sponge as I approached black belt testing. I practiced doing push-ups, anticipating the instructor would demand one hundred without stopping at testing. He customarily required fifty, but he knew that few would be no challenge for me. I could do seventy with ease.

Pull-ups and chin-ups were my favorite weight room exercises, and I did more than most males on any given day. I hated the bench press but wanted to work up to bench pressing my body weight. I read men's fitness magazines to learn how to get the most out of my workouts and to gain muscle. I worked with one male workout partner after another, as most people were inconsistent in the gym.

I trained to look strong and be strong. I did not want to be mistaken for a potential victim because of my small size; if anyone targeted me as a victim, they would regret it. Counter-intuitively, TKD first teaches students to use the most overlooked weapon, their voice. Sound simultaneously frightens our opponents and forces air into our lungs to support the use of force.

The sound that is produced during the execution of power is

called a "kihop." Characters make the sound in martial arts fight scenes. In forms, kihops are required to accompany specified executions, and in sparring each time we strike with force. Many students habitually ignore the kihop, but I enjoyed it because it made complete sense to me, as I regretted silence. Fear of being heard stifled my resistance during sexual abuse. Having learned that quiet resistance is rarely useful, I kihopped loudly, strongly and fiercely - louder than my silence, stronger than the marginalization of my pain, and fiercer than the denial I chose. Every kihop validated my right to resist shrinking.

When I slowed down my workouts, the grief and depression took over. Thus, I worked out twice a day when possible. I refused to use any nutritional supplements, but ibuprofen became my best friend to relieve the constant soreness from all the physical activity. However, ibuprofen could not keep me well. I landed in the emergency room from dehydration and fatigue.

One night I woke Sentwali at 2:00 a.m. to tell him I did not feel well and passed out shortly after. This time I had no stomach cramps, diarrhea, or constipation. Still, Sentwali treated me for the usual fainting spell, placing a cold towel on my body after forcing me back to consciousness with a slap in the face. I could barely move my weak body as he went to the kitchen to retrieve something light for me to eat and drink. I consumed a small amount and lay back down while he returned most of the uneaten snack to the kitchen. He returned to the bedroom to find me unconscious again. He brought me back to consciousness and I vomited. When he tried to call 911, I lied to stop him because I did not want to go to the hospital. "I feel fine now." We lay back down and fell asleep for a bit, but not for long. I awoke feeling faint and shoved Sentwali to wake him just before I passed out a third time. He called 911 and I did not contest.

I had not wanted to disturb the children but, each time I lost consciousness my body became weaker and weaker. Around 4:30 a.m. the ambulance arrived from around the corner. The paramedics reported my blood pressure to be 54/44, with an equally low pulse. The head paramedic looked at my well-defined abs and protruding bicep muscles and concluded that my lean body made me susceptible to dehydration. Sentwali mentioned the intensity of my workout routine, and the paramedic expressed a tad less concern about my blood pressure when he knew I ran long distances.

Long-distance runners commonly have low blood pressure; perhaps mine had not dropped much below my normal. The paramedics carried me downstairs because I could not walk or stand on my own. My daughter peeked her head out of her room as we passed by, and I knew she would panic. My husband quickly went to calm her while the paramedics carried me. They began intravenous fluids in the ambulance because they could not transport me to the hospital with my blood pressure that low.

I spent the morning in the hospital getting more tests that confirmed no illness or disease. My only symptom, severe fatigue, caused no alarm for the doctors. The doctor attributed the fainting to dehydration and released me hours later when I felt strong enough to walk.

I followed up with my physician the next day. She reiterated the paramedic's observation that I needed more fat on my body. The number on the scale was misleading because my body mass consisted of more muscle, which weighs more than fat. Though the scale indicated a healthy weight range, a visual scan suggested otherwise. My doctor advised me to put on five pounds by adding salt, fat, and sugar to my diet. She wanted to ensure I would not attempt to add muscle by lifting more weights.

My visit with the cardiologist revealed a nonthreatening tiny pinhole in my heart and a slightly irregular heartbeat. However, my heart functioned well and did not cause the fainting. The cardiologist phoned the neurologist to make an appointment for an assessment of my brain activity, and the neurologist asked about the reason for the referral. When the cardiologist explained my situation, the neurologist declined an appointment and gave me a prescription instead. Without any neurological assessment, he deduced that if my heart did not cause the fainting, then my brain must be the culprit; only a malfunction of the heart or the brain can cause fainting. Since the cardiologist had ruled out the heart, the neurologist concluded my brain needed to be repaired. The medication would help my brain function properly.

I never filled the prescription because the doctor never presented to me any neurological cause of the fainting spells. I resumed my workout routine more carefully after a week of recovery, obliged to include pretzels, sour cherry balls, and ginger snaps as part of my dietary requirements. I made sure to hydrate.

hree years after my double promotion in TKD, I finally completed the remaining seven ranks of the colored belts and applied for black belt testing. I watched new members come and go within weeks or months as the training became more physically and mentally challenging. In martial arts, training takes no less discipline than earning a higher education degree. The wealth of information I accumulated about the use of power, fitness, and Korean history, not to mention the conditioning of my body, placed me in an elite category. Only three percent of the American population advance to black belt; three percent also earn a doctoral degree. However, less than one percent achieve both, as I had. I expanded my life of beating the odds and felt accomplished.

The first part of my TKD test required one hundred push-ups, as I had predicted. I had worked up to eighty in training. During testing, I remember feeling deep pain in my triceps at eighty-something. By ninety I could no longer feel my arms. I do not know if I just stopped and waited until the instructor finished counting, did half push-ups, or what, as the attempt became an out of body experience of dissociation. The instructor said I did all one hundred, but I think he wanted me to not worry about such a small part of the test, given my overall success.

I impressively executed all nine forms and broke through the wooden boards with the required hand and foot techniques. I demonstrated sound self-defense techniques and knowledge of power. I also successfully sparred three opponents at once with well-controlled defensive and offensive strategies to pass my test with flying colors.

One week after I received my black belt, my sister Bernice rang to deliver the news about the death of Gwen's husband. This time, I received the call on my cell phone while driving home from out of town. When she hung up, I immediately called a friend and asked her to stay on the phone with me for the hour ride to my house in order to feel safe driving. Although I anticipated the news, I hurt badly. Every death compounded the pain from the previous ones. We laid my sister's husband to rest a mere fifteen months after Danny and twenty-seven months after David.

I stayed in Philly for three weeks to support my sister. We asked the funeral home, tongue-in-cheek, if they gave "frequent dyers" family discounts. At least we maintained our sense of humor. The funeral home staff knew the routine, and we did as well. Thus, planning the funeral came easy. However, three deaths within three years took a toll on our family. I felt the worst for my sister, as she had buried her brother, son, and husband. I wondered how she held up so well; I wanted to fall apart. Then again, my family had mastered the art of looking OK.

The night of the funeral, some family and friends gathered at Gwen's house because we knew the night would be difficult. My two violators were notably absent, an advantage to gathering at my sister's house rather than my mother's. Family typically gathered at Gwen's home only by invitation. Neither James nor Robin spent much time with the family to be invited there.

Nonetheless, as it frequently occurs in a family filled with such secrets and silence, one of the violators received an invitation to the gathering. One of my nieces suggested to Bernice that she call her husband to join us. Games were always more fun with more people, my niece innocently suggested. My sister replied that her husband likely would not come out since he enjoyed his alone time. I felt comforted by her response; however, that did not last long. I could not believe the words that came out of her mouth next: "He'll come out if Rose calls him." She then requested that I do so. At that time, I would have given my life for my family, so just like that, I picked up the phone and asked him to play games with us. He came instantly. We sure did play games; I lost.

I did not choose silence, but felt forced into it by systems or made content with it by loved ones. The bigger I made violators and enablers in my world, the smaller I became. I honored the belief that family is more important than feeling. My sister revealed to me her strong willingness to protect a false family image, and each time I arrived at a crossroads, I could not choose me in the perversely intimate space.

I felt trapped by the promise of silence I had made to Bernice a decade ago. That agreement guaranteed I would never be alone, but the circumstances made me wish I was alone. The promise assured me I would always have someone to talk with, yet it rendered me mute. My vow of silence came beautifully wrapped on the outside but stored lies and deception on the inside, which left no room for me to breathe. Bernice used and hurt me. Feeling suffocated, I made an appointment with Rita when I returned home.

CHAPTER 64

My husband and I barely spoke after the third funeral because I shut down. I loved him, but I despised him pretending he did not see my misery. I respected him, but resented his complacency with my life of silence. I did not trust him with my pain. I began to spend more time away from home because trauma filled every room in one way or another. Sentwali spent all of his time in the basement, so we rarely gathered in the same part of the house. When we were together, silence filled the room.

We never stopped touching, even when we stopped talking. He still held me selflessly until his arm went numb or massaged my body from head to toe with no demand, and I leaned into his gentleness. Making love reminded me of the beauty of partnering. His touch spoke a language my heart understood; his reverence for my body assured me of his love; his intentionality of offering me pleasure drew me in for an hour, sometimes two. He approached my body with the passion of an artist as if he saw me as the canvas; every stroke of the hand mattered. He placed his lips with the similar care of choosing the right color, and his full lips filled me with pleasure to compel my flesh to respond as he painted me in three-dimension to bring me to life. Thus, even if I died a thousand times, his laying on of hands would let me breathe again.

I tried to talk with Sentwali about our relationship, adding that I suffered emotionally from processing the abuse. He accused me of using the childhood trauma as an excuse to be selfish and expressed suspicion about me of having an affair. I understood his mistrust, as I spent quite a bit of time with men because of my fitness indulgence. But I had no interest in having an affair in my state of mind, and saw men mostly as sexless. I looked for all their endearing qualities that had nothing to do with their penis, but I could not convince my husband of my innocence. I admitted I enjoyed hanging out with my growing fan base of men. They showered me with more attention than Sentwali, but an affair would offer me nothing, as I desired to decrease the chaos in my life, not create more.

I reminded Sentwali that he knew about my sexual abuse before we were married and insisted on being with me despite my suggestion to break up. He replied that he had made a mistake. "We should have never married." He pummeled me with another emotional gut-punch. Three days of absolute silence passed between us, and I told him how much his comment hurt me. He tried to explain that he did not mean it the way I took it. He valued me as his wife but did not expect so many problems to evolve as a result of the abuse. He confirmed my belief that the more perfect I appeared, the more people supported me. I knew trauma and how to hide my wounds. I did not know how to express pain and to make everyone around me comfortable at the same time. I wanted to practice authenticity and transparency, but I could not do it without people distancing themselves from me or regretting their involvement with me.

I felt trapped, insignificant, abandoned, and unlovable. I

wished I could find comfort in the arms of another man. I surely would have if I thought for a second I could trust any man; but I did not trust a damn one. I wished I could ask for a divorce and simply walk away, but my fear of fainting alone overrode my need for validation. Instead, I numbed out more.

I called my mentor and friend, Dr. Cynthia Tyson, as we had kept in close contact since my doctoral graduation. We talked usually once every few months. She answered the phone to me crying and I continued for about two minutes before I could speak in complete sentences. I disclosed to her the sexual abuse for the first time and that I occasionally saw a therapist. I described Sentwali's response as insensitive and avoidant as she listened.

Dr. Tyson finally offered feedback, first commending me for seeing a therapist as she understood Black people tend to avoid seeking professional help for emotional issues. She then explained how much her heart ached from listening to me sob on the phone. She told me she felt helpless and my desperate cry triggered a profound sense of vulnerability within her. She saw me as one of her heroes, and knew few individuals as smart and strong as she had known me to be. If I could not make it in this world, then no one could.

She asked me to re-interpret Sentwali's response, remarking "No one who loves you can watch you in this kind of pain." Dr. Tyson suggested I consider that Sentwali could not help me deal with my pain because he could not deal with his helplessness. His own internal discomfort prevented him from sitting with mine.

Dr. Tyson also confessed that she put the phone down to avoid hearing me cry for such an extended time. She could not bear the deep pain coming from me and could only imagine how Sentwali must feel not knowing how to comfort me. She reiterated that no one who loved me could tolerate seeing such depth of my sorrow. She urged me to continue to see the therapist, as I needed to heal with the support of someone who could sit with me in the depth of my pain. She insisted that I go back to see Rita. I agreed that no matter what Sentwali said or felt, he took good care of me and treated me as well as he knew how. He always apologized for not knowing how to make me happier. I knew he wanted to make me happy, but I resented him for not wanting to carry my pain.

CHAPTER 65

$\mathcal{I}$ walked into my 3:30 p.m. appointment with Rita and did not make it five feet to the chair before I began to sob again. I immediately regressed and could feel all the pain of my seven-year-old-self spring up inside me before the session could officially begin. I could not hold back; I could not stop a single tear. Rita tried to talk to me, but I could not respond with words, only more tears. Tissue after tissue, I sank deeper and deeper into a spell of uncontrollable weeping. I could not breathe through my increasingly stuffy nose and could barely catch my breath as my head throbbed from congestion.

Fifteen minutes of unrelenting weeping led Rita to respond to my state of regression to my seven-year-old-self. "Rosenna, can you hear me?" She did not wait for a response, stating that she wanted to offer me a position she had never suggested to an adult client before but thought it might help. I nodded affirmatively, and she invited me to sit on her lap. I responded with a loud outburst of sobs as I moved toward her.

I will never forget her care at that moment as she guided me onto her lap, her body frame being not much larger than mine. She stroked my hair and held me like the seven-year-old I had regressed to unwillingly. She whispered sweet somethings in my ear and just let me cry it out. When I finally spoke, I still refused to leave her lap. I talked on her lap for the last fifteen minutes of our session after spending thirty minutes just crying.

When I left my session with Rita, I wondered how many adult survivors of childhood sexual abuse had never cried. I never cried as a child. I feared, acted out, got high, and got sick, but I never cried. Now I could not stop crying. I hardly left the house for weeks because my eyes stayed puffy. I spent more time in my room so the children would not see me crying. Unable to turn off the faucet of tears, I began regularly taking three nighttime pain relievers to get four hours of sleep.

I listened to my favorite meditation by Deepak Chopra while waiting to fall asleep. The meditation guided me through five activities to raise internal awareness. One part involved a request to focus on a happy memory from childhood. I disliked it because I could think of nothing pleasant from childhood. Eventually, I moved my focus to something else during that section and leaned into the remaining messages about purpose, intention, relaxation, and mantras.

Another sobering talk with Sentwali revealed his worry for my mental health, expressing concern about my ability to care for our children. He did not know if he could trust me with them, and I confirmed that he should not feel comfortable leaving me with them. For the first time, I mentioned my will to die: "I don't want to be here." I don't remember his response because I don't believe I heard it or cared. I only remember my tears.

I began to tell my closest friends about the abuse; they were empathetic listeners but offered nothing to relieve my pain. I found it difficult to describe the hurt to them, but the more I talked, the less I cried. One friend immediately picked up on my desire to create a masculine body type to avoid the interest of men. She, sarcastically referred to me as the stupidest smart person she had ever met, and assured me that I could not hide my beauty behind muscles. In spite of what I wanted to believe, men found me attractive and sexy, at the gym and everywhere else.

My friend urged me to stop wearing my daughter's clothing and buy an adult, unapologetically beautiful outfit for my head-turning physique that I had worked so hard to build. Occasionally, women would catch me at the drinking fountain or in the locker room and ask for advice. Before I could respond, they would interject, "But I don't want to look like you," meaning they did not want their muscles to protrude. I assumed most men were equally put off by my muscles. My friend assured me men were turned on by my body type, not turned off. My friend's advice transformed me into a fitness diva, investing in an entirely new fashion workout wardrobe that, admittedly, felt more comfortable.

I asked my sister Gwen to visit me for Christmas so she would not have to be in her house without her husband for her first Christmas alone. I refused to go to Philly, so she would have to visit me. I told Gwen I had been struggling with grief, and her presence would mean a lot to me. From the moment she arrived with her daughter I felt space around my pain and could breathe easier.

Stephanie, my sister's daughter, played well with my children. Gwen and I tried to talk about pleasant experiences rather than all the grief. We watched plenty of movies because Iowa did not offer much entertainment. The town centered around sports, but no one in my house ever cared about who won the Iowa versus Iowa State competition in any sport, not even my husband, an avid sports fan. Gwen and Sentwali watched professional football together. Gwen got along well with Sentwali since she catered to his interest in watching sports. They talked a lot, and I frequently joined in the conversation. Sentwali and I began to mend our relationship by accommodating Gwen and Stephanie. The six of us did as much as possible to bond.

Gwen expected to stay two weeks, but I pleaded with her to stay longer. I told her I feared my depression would return when she left, and I did not know if I would make it out of that dark space again if it returned. We cried together for a long time before she agreed, asking if I would be OK if she left and came back in a few weeks. I said no, I would not; I needed someone to support me. She understood and agreed to stay indefinitely.

Gwen called several people in Philly to make arrangements to take care of her house and car, conveniently located only a mile from our mother's house. She also made arrangements for one of our uncles to drive Danny's Mustang to Iowa so I could have it. She had been holding onto it because she could not bear to sell or drive it herself. She decided to give it to me to show appreciation for serving as his godmother. I had never received a gift so generous, in more ways than one; but her decision to stay with me meant the most. Finally, someone had chosen me.

After all of the arrangements were finalized for Gwen and Stephanie to remain with me in Iowa I felt safe enough to disclose to her about all of the abuse. I told her everything, and she replied she knew nothing about any of it. She recognized the need for Bernice to portray a life of perfection, but avoided criticizing her because the two of them had a close bond. Gwen thanked me for telling her what had happened to me and understood why I did not want to go back to Philly.

CHAPTER 66

*G*wen and Stephanie liked being away from Philly, although they had to adjust to the Bakari way of life, which included watching much less television and more quiet time in the house. We spent a lot of time at the gym, so Gwen and Stephanie picked up a fitness routine as well. We did not go to church anymore, but I knew Gwen would never live in a place where she had no church home. Respectfully, I took her to church a few times to get her acclimated, then stopped attending. My family did not eat red meat or pork, so Gwen cooked food for her and Stephanie when she had an appetite for those meats. I could tell Gwen got homesick quite a bit. Nevertheless, she chose me.

Having Gwen around also allowed me to travel with my husband. I desired more intimate time with him now that we had restricted personal space. He took the students on a two-day trip to a leadership conference. I found the topic of leadership valuable, so I attended the workshops as well. The keynote session opened up with a poet. I had begun to write poetry regularly after David died, feeling that journaling had failed me in moving from a place of despair. Looking at my journal entries over the years reminded me of unhappiness. I could tell no difference in what I had written a year ago from what I wrote yesterday; it all sounded the same. One day I decided to write poems rather than journals. I had written poems to help me sort through my feelings after the death of Pam and my father. I found they made for better processing and keepsakes. When I heard the poet at the conference, however, I experienced true transformational poetry for the first time.

The poet orated for seven minutes in rhythmic prose about growing up with a physically abusive mother. His passionate expression of pain and sorrow moved me. He spoke of dysfunctional family values of secrecy and lies and the resulting distorted perception of love. His noted desire for his mother to see how much he needed her lodged in my throat as if I had taken too big a bite of a sandwich. My eyes watered as my ears fixated on his every word, craving his ability to speak so freely about pain. I approached him afterward for his business card and asked for permission to contact him.

I called the poet about a week later and told him his poem had moved me. I mentioned that I had a traumatic experience of childhood sexual abuse but never wrote a word about it in my collection of over fifty poems. I wanted him to tell me what to do to release my trauma on the page in the same way he had done. He told me to sit down and write until the pen stopped, not my mind. I needed to "write beyond my mind." I found the conversation only slightly helpful in that I had told one more person my secret. Every time I disclosed, keeping the secret became less meaningful. However, he had not told me how to write about my pain.

The next day, I thought I would try to "write beyond my mind." I waited until evening when no one would disturb me. In my frequent sleepless state of mind, I picked up my pen and paper and began to write. Nothing about the abuse came out. I started writing about the phrase, "God made man in his image," and the harm men do to women in the image of God. I ranted about pedophiles, domestic violence, and rapists who take advantage of the system of female oppression. Finally, three pages into the poem I wrote my first words about my sexual abuse:

> *"I already survived rape at the age of seven*
> *Was that supposed to be my ticket to heaven*
> *Once I stopped wavering between insanity and suicide*
> *And refused to be the object of a man's warped sense*
> *of pride"*

My hands began to tremble when I wrote those words. I felt short of breath for a few seconds from my disbelief of the words on the paper but continued to write for another page and a half. I transitioned to urge women to claim their right to bodily autonomy and emotional independence.

I cried at the end of the poem because I could not release more about my sexual abuse. I intellectualized and externalized the pain. I wrote over five pages and made only four lines personal. On the other hand, I had written my first transformational poem, a poem written expressly to change the hearts, minds, or behaviors of its listeners, including the author.

CHAPTER 67

$\mathcal{M}$y mother and sister missed having Gwen around, and I felt slightly guilty about stealing her away. Bernice decided to visit us. I looked forward to seeing her in the safety of my home. We began making plans for things to do and, about a week before her arrival, she called to tell me she would be coming alone. She explained with disappointment that her husband would be unable to take off work to come with her. Perhaps he could come next time, she settled. When she stated that she had invited her husband into my home an ice-cold chill ran through my body and left a painful numbness. "OK," I eked out, astounded that she would invite him into my home, and relieved he declined her invitation.

I thought my heart and my head would explode. I knew I could no longer allow my Bernice's tasteless denial to torture me. I obsessed about her intention and wondered if she dangled me in front of him as bait to keep his attention. Did she forget everything I told her about what her husband had done to me? I even wondered whether Bernice envied me and wanted to hurt me for taking Gwen away from her. I had no rational explanation as to why she would try to bring her husband into my home and no longer wanted to see her. She did not belong in my house if she would not consider visiting without her husband. I knew I had to disconnect from her completely.

Bernice arrived as scheduled and stayed five days. I hardly said two words to her the entire time and could not stand to look at her because I felt too small. I regressed to my seven-year-old emotion of silence, feeling the deja vu of the little sister getting raped on the couch and the big sister hiding upstairs. I stayed in my space of silence, and she lived in her scope of denial. I let Gwen entertain Bernice and waited anxiously for her to return to Philly.

The day after Bernice left I went into Gwen's room to talk to her, sharing how I felt about Bernice's visit and my resentment about carrying the secrecy of the abuse. Gwen heartlessly and blatantly told me I had better get over it and move on with my life because that is what everyone else did. "Get over it": three little words crushed me like an elephant stepping on an ant it does not even know exists. I could not understand how she would say something so insensitive after responding with such care when I disclosed the truth. I thought she had chosen me, but she had not. She had decided to love me, but not to hear me.

I let out a scream only an insane person should release because I felt crazy. Gwen's response hurt so much. How did I ever shrink so small to fit in such a tiny space? I walked out of her room, slammed the door, and went into my room to lie down to cry. Everyone in the house ignored me and my sobbing.

For the next three days, my brain buzzed; I thought incessantly about the abuse, all of my disclosures, the therapy sessions, my husband's uselessness, my will to die, and my deep-seated sense of insignificance in the world. I lay in bed for the fourth sleepless night with all of it on my mind. Tylenol, meditation, reading, watching TV, nothing stopped the voices that were arguing in my head louder and louder. Each required something I could not give, a voice. I wanted the internal noise and pain to stop. Anxiety took over as I sat on the edge of insanity listening to the voices as if they were children playing beneath my bedroom window on a hot summer night with no air conditioner, forcing me to keep the window open.

I got out of bed to avoid letting out another scream. I did not want to awaken Sentwali, but he heard me go into the bathroom. I lay on the floor in the cramped bathroom balled up in a fetal position and let out only a whimper. My mind seemed to dissociate, and I did not know how to come back. I could not detach from the voices inside my head and the moans coming from my mouth as I lay on the floor. My world seemed as small as the cramped bathroom, so I might as well stay there. I had no reason to return to sanity.

Sentwali attempted to come in, but my body blocked the door. He asked if I wanted him to get Gwen. The question released me from my whimper and made me burst into tears as I wept, "No." He lay back in bed and waited for me to come out. In the fifteen to thirty minutes I lay there, I realized something had to change if I was ever going to leave the bathroom.

One of the voices in my head became clearer than the rest. It demanded, "You have to live openly." Yes, I needed an answer; that one felt right. I promised myself I would do whatever I needed to heal and would not reach fifty years of age carrying the pain of a seven-year-old. I stood up, still half-dazed but fully aware, perhaps for the first time in my adult life. I lay back down next to my husband and told him I needed to live openly. He said, "OK" and wrapped me in his arms.

he morning greeted me with confusion and frustration. Something vast had changed within me the night before on the bathroom floor. I could feel it but not identify it. I had heard tales of women giving birth in the bathroom and felt that is what I had done.

I knew I would never again share physical space with the men who violated me, even if it meant never going to Philly or inviting my mother and sister to my home. Because I valued my sister's friendship and wanted my mother's acceptance, I knew I had to choose freedom over family by allowing the pain of letting them go in order to save myself. I had to release the expectation that my family would ever rescue me from my pain. As much as I tried to love my sister and mother, which was too much, it would never be enough. I needed to prepare to spend holidays with Sentwali's family only, refuse invitations to family affairs and send birthday gifts through the mail to my mother.

I avoided confrontation because I had to sort through too many feelings and lean into the pain of my denial. I did not want to share any of my pain with my sister or mother or the violators.

I refused to seek validation of my pain or ask for affirmation of their love. They could not be a part of my healing journey. I no longer wanted to protect them; I needed to protect me. I did not want their version of the truth, knowing it would be different from mine because I had spent too many years living their version. I faded away from the family, which seemed to be a natural mourning from all of our losses, with fewer phone calls and shorter conversations.

I told Gwen I planned to live openly about the sexual abuse and would never return to Philly as long as James lived with our mother and Bernice remained married to Robin. Gwen did not want to see me disturbed again, so she just listened and kept the conversation short, careful to avoid judgment of my decision. I accepted her approach, for we needed each other too much. Although we spent little time together, we did what we could to support one another. We planned a trip to Orlando with the children for spring break to connect as a family.

While on the trip, I called each of the children into my bedroom one by one, Nailah, Gelani, and Stephanie, to disclose to each that James and Robin had sexually abused me in the past. I told them the violators' ages and mine at the time of the abuse. I did not offer any other details except my age when I told my mother and sister about the abuse. I asked them if anyone in the family had touched them. I apologized for placing them in an environment with people who had a history of harming children. Each assured me they had never been molested or damaged in any way.

I also wanted my children to know we would no longer participate in any family events because I refused to share space with James and Robin. Only my daughter, Nailah, asked me any questions. To my surprise, she asked why I had stayed with my family so long if they had treated me so wrong. I responded that I thought I needed my family but now realized I did not. In her adolescent wisdom she responded, "I've only known for twenty minutes, and I could have told you that you didn't need them. What took you so long?" She cried and I laughed and cried as I commented on her mature brilliance.

The Orlando vacation did us all good. I returned with no family secrets from my children and knowing they felt safe and valued. Gwen and I laughed with the children at the family outings and made their time special. I wanted to hold onto my relationship with her because of the uncertainty of my future family relations. However, I vowed to never talk to her again about the abuse.

I needed to keep talking in order to process my past, present, and future. As I could not speak about the abuse with anyone in the house, I called a friend I had recently met at a poetry event. She had recited a poem about her victimization of childhood sexual abuse and I could not help but introduce myself to her. We exchanged numbers and I called her after the Orlando trip.

I met my friend at her home to talk about my experience of abuse. She welcomed me and the conversation. I gave her the general information I had shared with the children, and she in return, delivered a fifteen-minute detailed account of what sounded like horrific childhood sexual abuse. She did not flinch with emotion. I wondered whether she recognized the absurdity of the behaviors of her caregivers. In my head I thought "That is some crazy shit." No wonder she had not told anyone all of it, as she had indicated to me.

For the first time in my life I decided to share the details of my experience because it appeared mild compared to what she had shared. I felt grateful that she lifted my burden of shame. I reciprocated by offering an extended rendition of my abuse. I disclosed my cousin giving me drugs, the fainting spells, the two years of molestation that went unnoticed even though it took place in the family home, and the fact that my sister knew of the abuse. I shared the responses of my mother and sister and how I bought gifts for violators and participated in holiday meals with them. I mentioned Bernice's request to keep the abuse a secret and her attempt to invite her husband into my home.

When I stopped talking, the look on her face mirrored my thoughts while she had spoken. She commented to me, "That shit is crazy." To our surprise, each of us had normalized our personal encounters of abuse. She felt the horror of my experience neutralized her shame. I could not believe how she felt and she could not understand my response to her. This "aha" moment showed me just how small the denial had made me, and I refused to remain that small.

I had suffered as an invisible victim of a hidden crime; no police record existed, no family outcry, and no neighborly concern. No one could see the scars on my body. The pinhole in my heart, asthma, arthritis, fibroids, and fainting spells tried to speak for me, but even I did not listen. By the time I finally spoke, no one knew how to respond to me as a victim.

Family members offered insulting advice to move on with my life. I tried for years; and if it had worked, this book would never have been written. I would have never mentioned the abuse to anyone. Telling a survivor to move on makes no more sense than saying to a cancer patient to have the chemo and just get back to work. Childhood sexual abuse is cancer to adult survivors. It kills many of us because we never find the healing path; some survivors do not know help even exists.

The complexity of childhood sexual abuse, including grooming, enabling, and dysfunctional family systems, fostered my silence. I did not have a simplistic story to tell, the one about the kidnapped child dragged into an alley by a stranger after school, or a teammate fondled by a coach after stepping out of the shower. I represented the eighty percent of child victims who experience sexual abuse at the hands of family members and the eighty-five percent of child victims who go unidentified during childhood. I lived from the age of seven to the age of forty-four feeling ashamed, insignificant, and unsafe in the world. The duration of time I lived in silence inversely related to my sense of personal significance. I arrived on the healing path an emotionally tangled mess, but I finally arrived.

CHAPTER 69

I began to search online for resources for adult survivors of childhood sexual abuse to support my healing journey. I could not afford to see Rita regularly, nor did I want any regular appointments. For as much as therapy costs, I found it too limiting. My pain stalked me daily, and I feared it. I woke up with anxiety and went to sleep with depression. I spent my day managing triggers. I avoided the news in case it reported a rape. I preselected movies I could watch with my husband to make sure they did not contain scenes of sexual violence. I steadily held back tears from leaning into the pain. Weekly therapy would not support my efforts to heal; I needed to build a daily support program for myself.

Unfortunately, I found no adequate outreach to help me process my experience. In 2007, to my surprise, "The Courage to Heal," a 1988 book, remained the most popular resource for survivors. I had not found the book helpful in my twenties and doubted it would support my healing journey in my forties. I longed for something that would address my willingness to deceive myself. I needed something that would address my internal struggle to put my needs before those of my family. I craved something to motivate me to live through my significance, rather than my fear of insignificance.

I found books geared toward therapists interested in helping survivors, but no books for survivors to help themselves. Two organizations online provided information about adult survivors, such as the average age of the onset of abuse, the average number of violators, and statistics related to the long-term effect. I became angry and confused when I learned that forty million adult survivors of childhood sexual abuse existed in America. How could the experiences of so many people like me be ignored? I cried with disbelief that I spent so much time feeling as though only I had experienced such horror. Forty million children could not be blamed for sexual abuse just because we became adults. I knew if I could discover what the forty million survivors did to heal, I could let go of my family.

I reviewed research journals to study the lives of the forty million survivors. Unfortunately, I found that many adult survivors of childhood sexual abuse and incest do not live well. They tend to live lives of silence like me. In fact, I realized I fared better than most and came to understand childhood sexual abuse as a risk factor for psychopathology, including post-traumatic stress disorder, addiction, eating disorders and depression.

I learned that adult survivors have more serious medical issues than those who did not experience childhood sexual abuse. I felt fortunate that none of my medical problems interfered with my daily life and I had managed to avoid obesity, as survivors' rates are twice as high. Survivors also have high rates of addiction, with forty percent females and sixty-five percent males reporting substance abuse.

As fortunate as I felt because I avoided these issues, I also felt at a loss on how to speak about my pain. I had no apparent evidence, and had intentionally designed a life that would leave no trace of childhood incest. I needed to find, define, and refine my journey of healing to live authentically and transparently, and to reclaim my dignity in order to live fully. I had to honor my right to heal, no longer choosing invisibility over ugly truths.

CHAPTER 70

I did not know how my future would unfold as I learned to live openly. I had no intention to announce myself as a survivor or to offer details about the abuse to everyone I befriended. However, I no longer had any purpose of keeping the abuse a secret either. I believed I would eventually learn how to create healthy boundaries instead of holding onto unhealthy secrets. I knew I had a lot to learn and process.

I continued to write poetry regularly as a way to process grief, racism, my children, love, and other emotions. I still had not written about the silence or sexual abuse, family dysfunction, or betrayal. I tried one more time. On March 15, 2007, I sat on my bed and put pen to paper to write beyond my mind. Hours later, the following poem presented itself to me as step one on my healing journey. Ready to live in my truth, I typed the poem and emailed it to my sister.

Too Much Love is not Enough
By Rosenna Bakari
March 15, 2007

I am enough/
Yes, I've been hiding and afraid for a long time/
Trying to keep dark secrets that torture my mind/
My voice was silenced, my mouth could not speak/
I had dark secrets I promised myself to keep/

I couldn't risk taking the blame/
I couldn't risk exposing the shame/
So I just accepted and played a deadly game/
Of make-believe and masquerade/
A lost shadow hidden by cold shade/

Forgive and forget, pray away your pain/
If you tell these dark secrets, there's nothing to gain/
All you'll do is make the whole family look bad/
There's no reason for everyone to feel sad/
So with my mouth shut wide/
    ...I hid all of those secrets deep down inside/

Do you know what happens to a child female mute/
She becomes prey for perpetrators calling her cute/
They smell her fear and are drawn to her silence/
That makes it easy for them to commit their violence/
They don't need a gun or even a knife/
A mute can't tell her mother and won't tell his wife/
But I kept hoping that they would see in my eyes/
That I was dying from carrying these heavy lies/
I was wavering between insanity and suicide/
Out of fear that my external perfection and self-hate
    would collide/

...After twenty years of anguish I finally spoke/
But the responses I received were little more than a joke/
Go ahead and do what you gotta do/

But not much I can do to support you/
A mother cannot turn her back on a son/
That was 20 years ago, what's done is done/
She did say she understood how I felt/
But we each had to play the hand we were dealt/

My cousin Larry was already dead/
The only solace placed upon my head/

My sister apologized for her husband's deeds/
But as his wife, she still had needs/
Please, little sister, don't say a word to anyone else/
Let's keep this secret on the shelf/
*   You know how much I love our son/*
He can never know what his father has done/

My mother and sister love me, so I thought they must
*   be right/*
So I picked back up my baggage and carried it into
*   the night/*
Where I watched them protect the men responsible for my
*   violation/*
While I silently wished for their castration/
I obey, I conform, I comply/
I keep moving to stay distant from the lie/
I bury my feelings in book after book/
I pay more attention to how my body looks/
Do anything not to feel/
Cause those dark secrets I promised not to reveal/

But within I feel victimized once more/
The demand for secrecy hurt me to the core/
I spend holidays with them, buy them presents and dine/
I make sure to smile so everyone thinks I'm fine/

Smart, pretty, thin, with plenty of success/
Surely it must be my silence that God has blessed/

They can't see my stomach in a knot/
My body remembers what my mind forgot/
Seizures, arthritis, fibroids, and fainting spells/
My body speaks what my mouth can't tell/
Running long miles and lifting heavy weight/
My body also tries to compensate/

No matter what I do the pain runs too deep/
These secrets are causing me too much pain to keep/
I make up stories about losing my virginity/
Cause the truth brings me no serenity/
Fetal position crying on the bathroom floor/
Trying to hold back emotions my mind doesn't want to
    explore/

Sometimes the universe puts the abuse right in my face/
And dares me to move from my silent space/
That's when I seek therapy to help me stay sane/
But I keep quitting because I can't take the pain/
Instead I keep searching for a rescue that never comes/
I'm stuck on a volcano island with a population of one/

I'm seven on the couch and 18 forced into bed/
30 to 40-year-old memories still fill my head/

Not a day goes by without deep regret/
And a silent prayer for their death that God neglects/
Maybe when their bodies are in the grave/
Their protectors will realize that I need to be saved/
But I'm the one dying so I can no longer wait/
Into my own hands my salvation I must take/

Despair finally reveals to me my own power/
I can choose the time, I can choose the hour/
I can take back my own voice/
I am responsible for my own choice/

The time has finally come that I choose me/
The time has come for me to set myself free/
No more stuffing hurt and lies/
No more hiding the tears I cry/

I will no longer allow you to keep these men in my life/
I don't care if you are his mother/
I don't care if you're his wife/
Don't ever again suggest bringing them into my home/
Don't ever think that I don't mind if we are left alone/

I don't want to know if they are sick or well/
There's nothing about them that I need you to tell/
I'm telling it to you in black and white/
I don't ever want them in my sight/
You have bonds with them you don't want to break/
But I must break my silence for sanity's sake/
My silence about the perpetrators and those who protect/
Those who asked me to simply forget/

But I never forgot and I never forgave/
I just kept waiting to be saved/
Waiting for someone to truly understand/
Waiting for someone to choose me over a man/
Waiting for someone to help me speak/
Waiting for someone to notice I was weak/
Waiting for someone to catch me when I fall/
Waiting for someone to help me stand tall/

Waiting for someone to notice the 7-year-old is still alive/
Waiting for someone to help her survive/
Even as I age and my beauty starts to fade/
I still found myself waiting to be saved/
But I remained a damsel in distress/
My abuse would forever go unaddressed/

Till a volcano erupted and I got caught in the fire/
That made me realize that silence is nothing to admire/
The singe of the fire forced me to scream/
Loud enough to wake from this very bad dream/
A three-time survivor of sexual trauma/
I couldn't get help from my own sister or momma/
So I lied and I cried and I covered my pain/
Till I had nothing to lose and everything to gain/
Disclosure will help my soul to restore/
Every day I love myself more and more/
The night is over, I can see day/
I walk and talk in truth's way/
Today anger fuels my recovery/
But that's all just part of my discovery/
Of the wounded child who is finally set free/
Who just learned to speak and she can finally see/

RESOURCES

Bakari, R. (2016). Original Sin: Understanding the Movement toward Female Empowerment. Karibu Publishing; Iowa.

Bakari, R. (2016). Tree Leaves: Breaking the Fall of the Loud Silence. Karibu Publishing; Iowa.

Bakari, R. (1994). Self-Love: Developing and Maintaining Self-Esteem for the Black Woman. Karibu Publishing; Wisconsin.

Bass, E., & Davis, L. (1988). The courage to heal: A guide for women survivors of child sexual abuse. New York: Perennial Library.

Boyd, J. A. (1997). In the company of my sisters: Black women and self-esteem. New York: Plume.

Bremner, J. Douglas et al. "Magnetic Resonance Imaging-Based Measurement of Hippocampal Volume in

Posttraumatic Stress Disorder Related to Childhood Physical and Sexual Abuse - A Preliminary Report." Biological psychiatry 41.1 (1997): 23-32.

Chopra, Deepak. (1994) Ageless Body, Timeless Mind: The Quantum Alternative to Growing Old. Harmony.

Chopra, Deepak. (2000) How to Know God. Running Press.

Darkness to Light Website: https://www.d2l.org/wpcontent/up loads/2017/01/all_statistics_20150619.pdf.

Gallo-Silver, Les, Christopher M Anderson, and Jaime Romo. "Best Clinical Practices for Male Adult Survivors of Childhood Sexual Abuse: Do No Harm." The Permanente Journal 18.3 (2014): 82-87. PMC. Web. 12 Dec. 2017.

Mountain Dreamer, Oriah. (1999) The Invitation. Harper San Francisco. ISBN 0062515845.

Musliner, Katherine L., and Jonathan B. Singer. "Emotional Support and Adult Depression in Survivors of Childhood Sexual Abuse." Child abuse & neglect 38.8 (2014): 1331–1340. PMC. Web. 12 Dec. 2017.

Rainn Website: https://www.rainn.org/articles/adult-survi vors-child-sexual-abuse.

Talking Trees, Inc., Website: https://talkingtreessurvivors .com.

Tolle, Eckhart: (2004) The Power of Now. New World Library.

Victims of Crime Website: http://victimsofcrime.org/
media/reporting-on-child-sexual-abuse/child-sexual-
abuse-statistics.

Wings Website: https://www.wingsfound.org

United States Department of Health and Human Services,
Administration for Children and Families, Administration
on Children, Youth and Families, Children's Bureau. Child
Maltreatment Survey, 2012 (2013).

U.S. Bureau of Justice Statistics. Sexual Assault of Young
Children as Reported to Law Enforcement. 2000.

ACKNOWLEDGMENTS

I wrote this book to paint a picture of a life of silence. As pictures are displayed in frames, I have used my marriage to frame my life of silence because the strength of my life with my husband has allowed me to do so. As he has come to know who I am, and who I am not, his love for me is resolute. I thank him for understanding my need to write every word. My love for Sentwali Bakari is beyond any word written on these pages.

I have met too many kind souls on my life journey to presume that I have achieved anything on my own. I have also met too many to list them all, though I am grateful for them all, from colleagues who supported my vision, to strangers who offered me sympathy and a warm smile. I have survived by sharing intimate emotional space with others, sometimes for brief periods, like workout partners to long-term mentoring relationships. Every interaction matters.

For more than five years I have communicated daily with my "Talking Trees: Adult Survivors of CSA" Facebook followers. Although I write daily posts to them, I always write for me. The safe space I created for survivors became the space I used to find my voice and to restore my soul. I thank each survivor who has chosen to walk the healing journey with Talking Trees since 2011, and those who will now join. I offer special gratitude to the "Talking Trees Branches" who push me beyond my comfort zone and stay ready to catch me if I fall. Thank you for helping me roar.

The words that appear on these pages have been subjected to many revisions, and this book could not have been possible without the input of many people. To name a few, Cathie Bryant (editor), Kerri Boehm (editor) and the relentless eyes of Gail Bernstein, Penny (Beagle) Green, Elaine Mattingly, Laurel Lewis, Audrey Voorhees, Linda Radtke, Tashema Cannon, and Meren Herbert. Thanks Jana Bussanich (photographer and cover designer) for extending extreme patience as well as professionalism. My organized team of supporters included, Elise Balcombe, Sandy Ho, Lizz Sharp, Emily Roesler, and Sara Almaraz.

I wish I could name each of the people who have helped me grow and chart my healing path in Colorado Springs over the past year by welcoming me and supporting my efforts to break the silence. To name only a few, Donna Nelson, Rodney Gullatte, Jr., Claudette Thompson Hutchinson, Tamara Moore, Anne Marie Pacitto, Sterling Chase, Liz Rosenbaum, Gloria Wilson Turnipseed, Shanyka Lock-Alcordo, Kristina Wright, Linda Weise, "Hot Comb" poets, and the Colorado Springs Business Journal.

SUPPORT THE MOVEMENT TO BREAK THE SILENCE

Breaking the silence of childhood sexual abuse is not a task. It is a journey of healing, a lifestyle of authenticity and a commitment to move humanity forward. You do not need to be a survivor of childhood sexual abuse to help us break the silence. You need only to create safe space for others to find their voice and design their path. You can help by doing any or all of the following:

1) Spread the word about this book. Each book sold represents a voice that is tired of living in silence.

2) Leave a review of the book on whatever media you can access online or offline.

3) Follow "Talking Trees Adult Survivors of CSA" on Facebook.

4) Go to Talkingtreessurvivors.com and sign up for the monthly newsletter.

5) Go to RosennaBakari.com and sign up for updates of forthcoming titles and other author activities.

6) Learn about "bodily autonomy" and "gene pooling." Writings about these concepts and theories can be found on my author page. They help frame the world epidemic of sexual abuse to

move from the individual to the collective, where there is safer space to heal.

7) Invite Dr. Rosenna Bakari as a professional speaker to your campus, company, or conference.

8) Heal one day at a time.

ABOUT THE AUTHOR

Rosenna Bakari is a scholar, motivational speaker, and social advocate. She is the founder and executive director of Talking Trees, Inc., an empowerment organization for adult survivors of childhood sexual abuse. When she started Talking Trees she had no idea that she would champion the cause through the telling of her own story.

Always enjoying writing more than reading, she published her first book about self-esteem in 1994 as a stay-at-home mother. Writing the current book became a necessity as part of her ten-year effort to invite survivors on the healing journey. Each of her four books targets the human spirit in one way or another since she uses her writing to support safe space for this sometimes-difficult life journey. She also has a transformational poetry collection of over one hundred and fifty pieces of work.

 facebook.com/1roguescholar

twitter.com/RosennaBakari

instagram.com/rosennabakari

amazon.com/author/rosennabakari

CPSIA information can be obtained
at www.ICGtesting.com
Printed in the USA
LVHW030529041220
673318LV00009B/1746

9 780997 169942